Secrets of the Kingdom Life

David Bercot

SCROLL PUBLISHING

Secrets of the Kingdom Life.

Scroll Publishing Co., P. O. Box 122, Amberson, PA 17210.
(717) 349-7033. www.scrollpublishing.com

Please contact us for a free catalog of our publications.

ISBN for printed edition: 978-0-924722-28-8

Printed in the United States of America

To my lifelong companion and best friend,

Deborah

Contents

SOME OF THE WEIGHTIER COMMANDS

1

The Mystery

God has given to man a short time here on earth, and yet upon that short time eternity depends. –Jeremy Taylor

The morning sun lit the sky, revealing a lone figure trudging along the narrow Tibetan path. When he had left the mountain valley before daylight, drizzling rain had been softly falling. This was unusual in October, for normally this was a dry month.

As the Christian missionary hiked along stony footpaths clogged with donkeys and goats, the rain fell harder. He pushed himself to walk faster. He knew that when he reached the higher elevations, the rain would turn to snow, and he had not come prepared for snow. He prayed constantly as he walked, asking God to protect him until he reached the safety of the rustic guest lodge that evening.

By noon he had reached an elevation of about 5,000 feet. He paused to take a drink and eat the bit of bread and cheese he had in his pocket. Below him lay a lush green landscape of fields dotted with small villages. He reflected for a moment on the various villages where he had spoken about Christ. He thought about the villagers dressed in their kaleidoscope of colors. He recalled the smiling faces of the children, running and playing.

Above him, four-mile-high peaks jutted up to the gray-white clouds. He dared not delay any longer, so he sprang up and continued his trek. He crossed a number of swinging footbridges that spanned deep ravines. On one of them he encountered another traveler. The Buddhist monk cut a striking figure in his saffron robe. Both men were headed to the same lodge, so they decided to walk together, single-file, with the monk leading the way.

On one side of the trail rose huge granite walls. Their pink and gray hues contrasted with the bright emerald moss growing in the cracks. The rain had turned to snow, and a bitter wind buffeted the men, who drew their cloaks tight to keep warm. Although neither man spoke, both knew they were in danger of freezing to death if they didn't reach the mountain lodge in time.

Suddenly they heard a voice. Both men stopped and looked around, but they saw nobody.

"Help," the voice called out weakly again. It seemed to come from a snow-covered rock on the side of the trail. But it was not a rock. It was a man lying on the trail, covered with snow. The missionary rushed to his side.

"What happened?" he asked.

"I fell off the ledge above," the man replied hoarsely. "I think I broke my ankle. I can't put any weight on it."

"Don't worry," the missionary reassured him. "We'll make a litter using my cloak, and we'll carry you to the lodge." He looked at the Buddhist monk as he spoke, hoping for confirmation.

But the monk shook his head. "There's no point in trying. If we attempt to carry him, we'll never make it to the lodge before dark. All three of us will end up freezing to death. Besides, without your cloak, you will freeze long before we reach the lodge. I wish there were a way to help this man, but there isn't." He then turned and continued on the path.

The missionary thought frantically. *What am I to do?* "Don't worry," he reassured the injured man. "I won't leave you here to die." He prayed for guidance. It seemed the only way to help now was to carry him piggyback. Thankfully, the hurt man was short and slender. The missionary stooped, and the man was able to climb onto his back.

The missionary lumbered down the path, slogging through the snow, praying for strength to continue the journey. Several hours passed. The weight on his back seemed to grow heavier and heavier with each mile. It was getting harder and harder to see as the daylight ebbed away. Finally, he thought he could go no further. He was tempted to unload his burden and go on alone. But just at that moment he spied the light from the lodge ahead.

With renewed determination, he plowed on. He had taken only a few steps more when he bumped into an obstacle in the path. He nearly lost his balance, but with great effort he regained his equilibrium. He gently unloaded the injured man onto the snow, reassuring him that it was only for a moment, and returned to the object he had nearly tripped over. It was the Buddhist monk. The missionary felt for a pulse, but the monk was dead.

The missionary hurried back to the injured man and helped him onto his back again. As they trudged on to the lodge, he contemplated what had happened. Why had the monk frozen to death while he had not? Suddenly it dawned on him—the injured man on his back! The heat from their two bodies together had kept both of them alive! The monk walking by himself had frozen to death in the bitter cold.

What a paradox! the missionary realized. By risking his life to save another man's, he had unwittingly preserved his own.

The Paradoxical Kingdom

Perhaps this missionary should not have been surprised at this paradox. For he belonged to a kingdom that is full of paradoxes. A paradox is something that is contrary to normal expectations. It seems self-contradictory, but actually is not. The kingdom of God is full of such paradoxes. Here are just a few of them:

- "The last will be first, and the first last" (Matt. 20:16).
- "He who finds his life will lose it, and he who loses his life for My sake will find it" (Matt. 10:39).
- "Blessed are the meek, for they shall inherit the earth" (Matt. 5:5).
- "Blessed are you when men hate you" (Luke 6:22).
- "I tell you not to resist an evil person. But whoever slaps you on your right cheek, turn the other to him also" (Matt. 5:39).
- "If anyone wants to sue you and take away your tunic, let him have your cloak also" (Matt. 5:40).
- "Whoever compels you to go one mile, go with him two" (Matt. 5:41).

The Great Paradox

Yes, to live the kingdom life is to live a life of paradoxes. However, one paradox has remained unfathomable to most Christians. I call it the Great Paradox. It concerns two teachings of Jesus about the Christian life that seem not only contradictory, but diametrically opposite.

In the first teaching, Jesus explains the enormous sacrifices we must make if we want to be His followers:

> If anyone desires to come after Me, let him deny himself, and take up his cross, and follow Me. If anyone comes to Me and does not hate his father and mother, wife and children, brothers and sisters, yes, and his own life also, he cannot be My disciple. And whoever does not bear his cross and come after Me cannot be My disciple.
>
> Likewise, whoever of you does not forsake all that he has cannot be My disciple. Strive to enter through the narrow gate, for many, I say to you, will seek to enter and will not be able. Matt. 16:24; Luke 14:26-27, 33;13:24 (condensed)

So to be disciples of Jesus, we must strive to enter through the narrow gate. We must deny ourselves, our families, and everything we own. In fact, we cannot hold back even our very lives. It would seem that being followers of Jesus is one of the most challenging quests we can face.

Yet Jesus also tells us: "Come to Me, all you who labor and are heavy laden, and I will give you rest. Take My yoke upon you and learn from Me, for I am gentle and lowly in heart, and you will find rest for your souls. For My yoke is easy and My burden is light" (Matt. 11:28-30).

How can both of those teachings be true? First Christ requires us to deny *everything*, including our own lives. Then He tells us that His yoke is easy and His burden is light. How can His yoke be easy if He requires us to deny everything and carry our cross?

The answer is to be found in the secrets of the Kingdom Life.

2

What Is The Kingdom Life?

Christianity does not consist in the fewness of our vices, but in such a thorough change of heart, as makes reverence and holiness the measure and rule of all our emotions. –William Law

Believe me, if you will but persevere you will be forced to confess that one single day of surrender is worth more than a thousand years of worldly life. –Francis of Sales

About a decade ago, I wrote the book, *The Kingdom That Turned The World Upside Down*, which describes the Kingdom of God and many of the Kingdom teachings of Jesus. In that book I mainly discuss the external commandments of this Kingdom—such as nonresistance, the permanence of marriage, and refusal to take oaths. Those are some of the laws of God's kingdom.

However, in this present work, we will be talking about Jesus and His kingdom totally possessing us. When I use the term, the Kingdom Life, I'm referring to something much deeper than just external obedience to Jesus' kingdom commands. Jesus revealed one of the secrets of the Kingdom Life when he said, "The kingdom of God is within you" (Luke 17:21).

The Kingdom Life is something that has to begin inside of us, and it must flow from the heart to the outward applications. In the pages that follow, we're going to be looking at the secrets that enable us to live this life. When I say "secrets," I don't mean that nobody else knows about the things I'll be sharing. Rather, I'm using *secret* in the dictionary sense of "a method known only to a few." Neither the world, nor nominal Christians, nor those who have bought into "easy believism" know anything about the Kingdom Life.

The Kingdom Life requires Jesus and His kingdom dwelling inside of us—changing and motivating us from the inside out. When we are born again, Jesus automatically comes to live inside of us. However, His *continuing* to dwell in us is not automatic. Jesus explained this when He spoke to the apostles at the Last Supper:

> I am the true vine, and My Father is the vinedresser. Every branch in Me that does not bear fruit He takes away; and every branch that bears fruit He prunes, that it may bear more fruit. You are already clean because of the word which I have spoken to you. Abide in Me, and I in you. As the branch cannot bear fruit of itself, unless it abides in the vine, neither can you, unless you abide in Me.
>
> I am the vine, you are the branches. He who abides* in Me, and I in him, bears much fruit; for without Me you can do nothing. If anyone does not abide in Me, he is cast out as a branch and is withered; and they gather them and throw them into the fire, and they are burned. If you abide in Me, and My words abide in you, you will ask what you desire, and it shall be done for you. By this My Father is glorified, that you bear much fruit; so you will be My disciples.
>
> As the Father loved Me, I also have loved you; abide in My love. If you keep My commandments, you will abide in My love, just as I have kept My Father's commandments and abide in His love. John 15:1-10

Here Jesus explains that the Christian life is one that requires an abiding or continuing relationship with Him. This abiding relationship is obviously not automatic or there would be no point to what He said. Whether or not Jesus remains in us depends upon our obedient response

---

* Abide means to remain, continue, or dwell.

to His love. "If you keep My commandments, you will abide in My love, just as I have kept My Father's commandments and abide in His love" (John 15:10). Jesus tells us there is an inseparable link between our obedience and our abiding or continuing in His love. Maintaining this link requires our surrender to Christ.

Gelassenheit

The German medieval spiritual writers used the term *Gelassenheit* to describe such self-surrender or total abandonment to God. In the sixteenth century, the Anabaptists espoused this term to describe the Kingdom Life. Anabaptist writer Hans Denk said, "There is no other way to blessedness than to lose one's self-will."[2] It was this *Gelassenheit*, this total surrender to God's will, that enabled the sixteenth-century Anabaptists accept the cross of imprisonment, torture, and often death.

Gelassenheit remained an important concept of the Anabaptists even after the age of persecution ended. The German Pietists also adopted the word to refer to total surrender to God and the joyful acceptance of His will. In short, the Kingdom Life can only be lived by Christians who have totally surrendered themselves to God. Such Christians live no longer for their own personal ambitions. They live wholly for Christ. They think of God in everything they do. They serve God in every way possible.

What I'm calling the Kingdom Life, spiritual writers in the past often called the Devout Life, the Surrendered Life, or Christian Perfection.* They all refer to the same thing, a life totally devoted to God. The Christian who lives the Kingdom Life sanctifies his daily life by doing

* By Christian Perfection, these writers do not mean that we can live a flawless life. They're using the word *perfection* in its original sense of "completeness."

everything in the name and spirit of Christ. His body may be on earth, but his mind is in heaven. George MacDonald, nineteenth-century Scottish pastor and spiritual writer, describes the Kingdom Life in these words:

> No man can have the consciousness of God with him and not be content. No man who has not the Father so as to be eternally content in Him alone, can possess a sunset or a field of grass or a mine of gold or the love of a fellow-creature according to its nature—as God would have him possess it.
>
> If you are not content, it is because God is not with you as you need Him to be with you. For you need Him more than your body ever needed food or air. You need Him as much as your soul has ever hungered after joy, peace, or pleasure. The person who loves his fellow man is infinitely more alive than he who tries to exalt himself above others.
>
> The person to whom God is all in all, who feels his life-roots hidden with Christ in God—this person knows himself to be the inheritor of all wealth, all worlds, all ages, and all essential power. This person has begun to be alive indeed. For he is in the image of God, and he is ready to partake of the life of the Most High and be alive as He is alive.

All of this goes back to Creation. We were made in the image and likeness of God. So we can only find true happiness and rest in God Himself and in the very things that God enjoys. In Genesis, God commanded every tree to bear fruit according to its kind. Today God asks the same thing of us: to bear fruit consistent with the image of God imprinted on our souls. Without Christ, we cannot possibly bear such fruit. But with Him we can bear an abundance of fruit.

Paul gives a perfect description of the Kingdom Life when he writes, "I have been crucified with Christ; it is no longer I who live, but Christ lives in me; and the life which I now live in the flesh I live by faith in the Son of God, who loved me and gave Himself for me" (Gal. 2:20).

Eighteenth-century English spiritual author William Law writes, "Would you know the blessing of all blessings? It is this God of love dwelling in your soul and killing every root of bitterness. For bitterness is the pain and torment of every earthly, selfish love. When we live in the spirit of love, all needs are satisfied and all disorders of nature are removed. Life is no longer a burden. Every day is a day of peace. Everything you meet becomes a help to you because everything you see or do is all done in the sweet, gentle element of love."[3]

John and the Kingdom Life

The apostle John describes the Kingdom Life when he writes, "This is the love of God, that we keep His commandments. And His commandments are not burdensome" (1 John 5:3). Most Bibles translate this passage as two separate sentences, as I've just quoted above. However, many Christians don't realize that in New Testament *koine* Greek there were accent marks but no punctuation marks—no periods, commas, colons, or quotation marks. So translators have to make judgment calls as to where to put punctuation marks. Perhaps the apostle John intended for this passage to read as two separate sentences.

However, I think it is more likely that he intended for the passage to say, "For this is the love of God: that we keep His commandments and His commandments are not burdensome." In other words, we know that we finally love God with our whole heart, soul, mind, and strength when we reach the point that we not only obey all of His commandments, but we also find that they are no longer a burden. At this point we've solved the Great Paradox. The Christian living the Kingdom Life lays down everything for God, totally denying himself. However, he is so in love with God that he finds such surrender the lightest burden anyone could carry.

Christians who live the Kingdom Life don't love God because the Bible commands them to, but because of the new nature inside their souls that reaches out to God in love. Likewise, they pray continually, read the Scriptures daily, and gives thanks in all things—not because God has commanded them to do so, but because their souls cherish being in constant communion with their beloved Maker.

Those living the Kingdom Life repent at once of their mistakes, sins, and follies. Again, this is not merely because Scripture commands them to, but because they recognize their spiritual needs and do not want anything to jeopardize their relationship with God. They know the misery of a sinful and spiritually barren life, and they have no desire to return to it.

Surprisingly, however, those living the Kingdom Life often don't have the support of their own brethren.

3

Naysayers and Half-and-Half Christians

Sadly, ever since the time of Constantine, Christians who have wanted to live the Kingdom Life have typically received most of their opposition from other church members—not from the world. In the first three hundred years of Christianity, living the Kingdom Life was the norm. Not everyone lived it, but no Christian was viewed as odd by his fellow believers for living such a life. Living the Kingdom Life meant going against the flow of the *world*, but not of the *church*.

However, in the fourth century, the church made enormous compromises with the world. As a result, before long, living the Kingdom Life meant going against both the world and the church. Living the Kingdom Life posed a grave threat to the status quo of religious mediocrity that enveloped the church. Back in the sixteenth century, Francis of Sales warned those who wanted to live the Kingdom Life, "They will predict your premature old age and the ruin of your material prosperity. They will tell you that in the world you must live as the world does; that you can be saved without all this fuss; and much more of the like nature."[4]

Today other Christians will label you as being legalistic or fanatical. They'll claim that you're no Christian at all because you're practicing "works righteousness."

They will try in vain to elevate their worldly life above your Kingdom Life. John Wesley made this observation:

> This is liberty, true gospel liberty: Not freedom from the law of God, or the works of God, but from the law of sin and the works of the devil. See that you stand fast in this real, not imaginary "liberty, wherewith Christ has made you free." Do not stupidly and senselessly call this legalism—a silly, meaningless word. Do not be afraid of being under the law of God, but of being under the law of sin.
>
> Allow me to warn you of another silly, meaningless phrase: Do not say, "I can do nothing." If so, then you *know* nothing of Christ; then you have no faith. For if you have faith, if you believe, then you "can do all things through Christ who strengthens you." You can love him and keep his commandments.
>
> And to you his "commandments are not grievous." Grievous to them who believe? Far from it! They are the joy of your heart. Show then your love to Christ by keeping his commandments, by walking in all his ordinances. Trust in Christ to live and reign in your heart.[5]

The Half-and-Half Christian

To live the Kingdom Life takes enormous faith. So most Christians go in only halfway. They give part of their life to God and keep part for themselves. They obey some of Christ's commands but ignore others. They reject half of what the world offers, but imbibe the rest. They are half-and-half Christians.

The anonymous author of *The Kneeling Christian* notes, "The half-and-half Christian is of very little use to either God or man. God cannot use him, and man has no use for him, but considers him a hypocrite."[6] Wanting to enjoy the benefits of both God and the world, such Christians miss out on both.

Half-and-half Christians can appreciate the fact that if we are totally absorbed in worldly pleasures, our lives will surely be empty. But they imagine that complete self-denial would make for a dull, miserable, melancholy existence. They realize that an excess of pride makes for a despondent life. However, they imagine that if they fully empty themselves and live in total humility, this would be a wretched life as well. The half-and-half Christian imagines he's getting the best of both worlds, when in reality he's getting neither.

A Salvation Unworthy of Our God

One of the problems is that so many Christians think of salvation only in *judicial* terms—being admitted into heaven and escaping eternal punishment. Obviously, we all want judicial salvation. However, mere judicial salvation is unworthy of our God. Jesus didn't come to earth merely to add Christian ordinances and theology to a non-surrendered life.

Christ wants to do more for us than simply admit us into heaven. He doesn't want to save us *in* our sins. He wants to save us *from* our sins. He wants to rescue us from our fallen nature and enable us to be partakers of His nature. He doesn't want to do this after we get to heaven, but *now*. His commandments are given to help us become more like Him and less like the world. That's what the Kingdom Life is all about.

If we find Christ's commandments burdensome *now*, we're going to find them burdensome in heaven. Now is when we must surrender to God, not after we die.

A Life of Joy

Nineteenth-century preacher Andrew Murray observed, "To many Christians the thought of a life wholly abiding in Christ is one of strain and painful effort. They cannot see that the strain and effort only come as long as we do not yield ourselves unreservedly to the life of Christ in us." Living the Kingdom Life is not like undergoing a prison sentence. In surrendering our lives to Jesus, we find true freedom and joy. It is only in the Kingdom Life that these words of Jesus find their ultimate fulfillment: "Come to Me, all you who labor and are heavy laden, and I will give you rest. Take My yoke upon you and learn from Me, for I am gentle and lowly in heart, and you will find rest for your souls. For My yoke is easy and My burden is light" (Matt. 11:28-30).

A few years ago, the German luxury carmaker BMW ran ads in various magazines that featured a picture of one of their beautiful sedans with a single word beneath it: *Gelassenheit*. Knowing this word only in the spiritual sense, I couldn't fathom what possible connection there could be between *Gelassenheit* and a luxury sedan. However, after digging further, I finally discovered that BMW was using the word to mean *serenity*. Ah, now I could see the connection. For the world, serenity is a BMW. For someone who loves God, serenity is the Kingdom Life.

To be sure, the Kingdom Life comes with many sacrifices. "We must through many tribulations enter the kingdom of God" (Acts 14:22). But the non-surrendered life brings far more woes. So much of human suffering and misery is caused by sin. At the Last Supper, Jesus warned His disciples about the persecution they would receive. Yet He also told them that living their lives for Him would bring great joy. "These things I have spoken to you, that My joy may remain in you, and that *your joy may be full*. . . . You now have sorrow; but I will see you again and your heart will rejoice, and your joy no one will take from you. . . . Until now you have asked nothing in

My name. Ask, and you will receive, that your joy may be full" (John 15:11; 16:22,24). Jesus specifically mentions joy four times in that combined passage.

The Kingdom Life is not a life free of sacrifice, but it is truly a joyful life. As strange as it seems, the more we deny ourselves, the easier Christ's yoke becomes. The only way to experience more of Christ's joy is to have more of Him, not less of Him. Carrying a heavy cross turns out to be a light burden. In fact, the answer to the Great Paradox is living the Kingdom Life.

The more of our lives we surrender to God, the more we partake of the Divine nature and live in accord with what God originally intended for mankind. The more we live in harmony with His goodness, the more content and thankful we are and the more joy we receive.

Early Anabaptist writer Leonhard Schiemer noted, "Worldly living starts out joyfully and ends in eternal sorrow. But our kind of living begins in sorrow. Then soon the Holy Spirit comes and anoints us with the oil of inexpressible joy."

Of course, it's fine to describe the joys and rewards of the Kingdom Life. But what we really need to know is *how* to live it. So let's start looking at some of the secrets to living the Kingdom Life.

4

Tapping Into God's Power

Men are everywhere crying and sighing for power and the fullness of the Spirit, but they neglect the means by which this power and fullness are obtained. –Samuel Logan Brengle

Unless our old man is really crucified with Him, the Cross of Christ will profit us nothing. –William Law

True victory over self is the victory of God in the man, not of the man alone. –George MacDonald

At the Last Supper, Jesus gave us one of the most illuminating explanations of the Kingdom Life in His illustration of the Vine, which we just read. Here Jesus explains that the Christian life is one of an abiding relationship with Him. Salvation is not a "once and done" operation. Furthermore, it's not just *any* relationship with Jesus, but a relationship that bears godly fruit. Or, to put it another way, it is an obedient love-faith relationship with Christ. According to Jesus, bearing godly fruit is essential, not discretionary.

The Kingdom Life can only be achieved through the power that Christ gives. Yet, that doesn't mean that we play no part in it ourselves. The first secret of the Kingdom Life is that it is built on two key spiritual truths:

- **Christ**: "Without Me you can do nothing" (John 15:5).
- **Man**: "I can do all things through Christ who strengthens me" (Phil. 4:13).

Christ tells us that we will never be able to produce fruit on our own strength—let alone live the Kingdom Life. We need to maintain a close spiritual relationship with Him. Most Christians are aware of that. However, too many Christians think that Christ's words mean, "I will do everything for you." But that's not what Jesus says.

A few years ago my wife and I decided to modify our diet to eat more fruits and vegetables. My wife bought a blender so she could easily make fruit smoothies and other whole food items. As long as the blender is unplugged from the electrical outlet, it doesn't work. It can't chop vegetables or liquefy fruit. Without electricity, the blender can do nothing. It is like a man without Christ.

Does that mean, then, that electricity does *everything?* Does it mean my wife didn't need to buy a blender after all? Of course not. Without electricity the blender can do nothing. But the electricity by itself can't chop vegetables or make smoothies. The electricity gives the blender the power it needs. With electricity, the blender can do amazing things.

The Christian life is the same. On our own strength, we can't live even a basic Christian life—let alone the Kingdom Life. Yet with Christ's power we can do all of the things He asks of us. Unlike the illustration of electricity, Christ actually *could* do everything for us. That is, if He wanted a bunch of robots to move about at His pleasure. But He doesn't want robots; He wants warm humans who choose to obey Him because they love Him. Christ won't do our obeying for us. He requires our participation in bearing fruit and living the Kingdom Life.

So what part does God play, and what does God require of us?

What God Does for Us

To begin with, God gives us the new birth. As Jesus said, "Most assuredly, I say to you, unless one is born of water and the Spirit, he cannot enter the kingdom of God" (John 3:5). Nobody can give the new birth to himself. It has to come from God. And without the new birth, we can't enter the kingdom of God. No wonder Jesus tells us that without Him we can do nothing. We can't even *begin* the Christian life without Him. In fact, Jesus explains that we would never originally have taken any steps toward Christ, if God had not worked in our hearts. "No one can come to Me unless the Father who sent Me draws him" (John 6:44).

Paul tells us that the Father "has delivered us from the power of darkness and conveyed us into the kingdom of the Son of His love, in whom we have redemption through His blood, the forgiveness of sins" (Col. 1:13-14). Through Christ our sins are forgiven, and we are redeemed through His blood. Without Christ and His Father, we would remain trapped under the powers of darkness. We can't force our way into the kingdom. God conveys us there.

Once we are redeemed, God continues to work in us. Paul told the Ephesians, "For this reason I bow my knees to the Father of our Lord Jesus Christ, from whom the whole family in heaven and earth is named, that He would grant you, according to the riches of His glory, to be strengthened with might through His Spirit in the inner man, that Christ may dwell in your hearts through faith" (Eph. 3:14-17). So the Father "strengthens us with might through His Spirit," and Christ "dwells in our hearts through faith" to provide us continuing power.

Paul didn't say that through his own power he could do all things. Rather, he said, "I can do all things *through Christ* who strengthens me" (Phil. 4:13).

What God Requires of Us

God transforms us into a branch on the Vine of His dear Son and infuses us with divine power. Having done that, God expects us to respond to that power. He requires us to cooperate with Him in producing godly fruit.

Seventeenth-century Scottish minister Henry Scougal writes, "The Holy Ghost must come upon us and the power of the Highest must overthrow us, before that holy thing can be begotten and Christ is formed in us. Yet we must not expect that this whole work should be done without any concurring endeavors of our own. . . . We must not lie loitering in the ditch and wait till Omnipotence pulls us from there. No, no. We must bestir ourselves and actuate those powers we have already received."[7]

That's exactly what Scripture teaches. Paul exhorts us, "I beseech you therefore, brethren, by the mercies of God, that you present your bodies a living sacrifice, holy, acceptable to God, which is your reasonable service. And do not be conformed to this world, but be transformed by the renewing of your mind, that you may prove what is that good and acceptable and perfect will of God" (Rom. 12:1-2).

Paul says that *we* must present our bodies as living sacrifices that are holy and acceptable to God. *We* must not conform ourselves to this world. *We* must allow ourselves to be transformed. All of this is through the "mercies of God" and His transforming power. So it is a matter of our cooperating with the working of the Spirit.

Paul writes further, "The grace of God that brings salvation has appeared to all men, teaching us that, denying ungodliness and worldly lusts, we should live soberly, righteously, and godly in the present age" (Tit. 2:12). Without the grace of God, we would never get on the Vine to start with or be able to produce fruit. Yet that same grace teaches us that *we* have to deny "ungodliness and worldly lusts." *We* have to "live soberly, righteously, and godly." Again, it is a matter of man cooperating with the power of God that works within him.

Peter exhorts us, "Gird up the loins of your mind, be sober, and rest your hope fully upon the grace that is to be brought to you at the revelation of Jesus Christ; as obedient children, not conforming yourselves to the former lusts, as in your ignorance; but as He who called you is holy, you also be holy in all your conduct, because it is written, 'Be holy, for I am holy' " (1 Pet. 1:13-16). Once again, the Scriptures make it clear that in response to God's grace, God expects us to be sober, to be obedient, and to be holy. The power comes from Him; the sacrificial response must come from us.

The early Christian teacher Clement of Alexandria explains it this way, "A man by himself working and toiling at freedom from sinful desires achieves nothing. But if he plainly shows himself to be very eager and earnest about this, he attains it by the addition of the power of God. God works together with willing souls. But if the person abandons his eagerness, the Spirit from God is also restrained. To save the unwilling is the act of one using compulsion; but to save the willing, that of one showing grace."[8]

God and the Farmer

Living the Kingdom Life is like farming. Without the things that God supplies, a farmer can do nothing. Think of all the things that God provides for the farmer. God furnishes the earth itself, without which the farmer would have nothing to plant his seeds in. And the seeds would have nowhere to send their roots to obtain water and nutrients. God provides the water—whether through rain or from irrigation. God supplies the sun, without which nothing could grow. The very seeds the farmer plants are distant offshoots of the original plants created by God. We can truthfully say that without God, the farmer can do nothing.

Does that mean that God does everything? Can the farmer just sit back and wait for God to grow his crops for him? Anyone who farms or gardens knows all too well that it doesn't work that way. A lot of hard work is involved in farming. The farmer has to plow his field; God won't plow it for him. The farmer has to plant the seeds; God won't plant them for him. The farmer has to apply fertilizer and fight weeds and pests. God doesn't do those things for him. Finally, the farmer has to harvest the crop. God won't do that either.

Yes, without God, the farmer can do nothing. But God makes the farmer earn his living by the "sweat of his brow." God and the farmer are partners. It's the same way in the Christian life—man cooperating with God.

God and the Olympic Athlete

The Scriptures sometimes liken the Christian life to an athletic race: "Therefore we also, since we are surrounded by so great a cloud of witnesses, let us lay aside every weight, and the sin which so easily ensnares us, and let us run with endurance the race that is set before us" (Heb. 12:1). Paul uses the same analogy in his first letter to the Corinthians: "Do you not know that those who run in a race all run, but one receives the prize? Run in such a way that you may obtain it" (1 Cor. 9:24).

Did you notice that in both texts, the writer says that it is *we* who run the race. God does not run our race for us. Does that mean we can run the race of life on our own power? No, of course not. The power has to come from God.

Probably no one has understood this joint relationship of God and man better than Paul. He knew that without Christ, he was nothing. Yet he also knew that he had to exert himself if he was going to run this race faithfully until the end. Remember his words: "But I discipline my body and bring it into subjection, lest, when I have preached to others, I myself should become disqualified" (1 Cor. 9:27). If Paul was concerned about being disqualified, how much more so should we.

But can we fully embrace the Kingdom Life overnight? Is it an instant thing like the new birth?

5

A Gradual Process

Little and small matters are the first steps and natural beginnings of great perfection. –William Law

Our change will be so gradual that the world will still suppose us to be Esau, when we really are Jacob. –Francis of Sales

Because God requires our cooperation, coming to the Kingdom Life is not an overnight process. God wants our willing hearts. He will not force us into a Kingdom Life against our will. Few of us surrender our own will all at once, so the process is a gradual one. It's like the break of day—the sun doesn't overcome the darkness all at once, but by degrees.

It's a pity that "salvation preaching" rarely includes explanations like this. When giving a salvation message, evangelists often bring forth testimonies that give their listeners the impression that enormous changes will automatically take place upon their conversion. While it's true that conversion often brings about radical changes in a person's life, it almost never instantaneously transforms an unsaved person into one who is living the Kingdom Life. No, one of the secrets of the Kingdom Life is that it's a gradual growth process that requires substantial discipline and self-denial.

J. C. Ryle, a nineteenth-century evangelical preacher, made the following observation: "There are some of the Lord's people who seem never able to advance and grow from the time of their conversion. They are born again, but they remain babies all their lives. They are learners in Christ's school, but they never seem to get beyond their ABCs. They have gotten inside the fold, but there they lie down and go no further. Year after year you see in them the same old habitual sins. You hear from them the same old experience."[9]

Actually, to a large degree, Ryle's words describe the typical Christian today. Many new converts experience growth during the first year or two after their conversion. But often they reach a plateau where they remain the rest of their lives. As Ryle described, "You see in them the same old habitual sins. You hear from them the same old experience."[10]

So it's important to remember that the Kingdom Life is not automatic, and it doesn't happen all at once. We shouldn't be discouraged that the Kingdom Life doesn't come to us easily. We should expect setbacks, but we shouldn't let them discourage us from continuing in our surrendered walk. Satan will want to use our failings and setbacks to convince us to give up. He wants us to think that we're spiritual failures when we fall back into old habits or when we fail tests that come our way.

With that in mind, we're ready to look at the other secrets of living the Kingdom Life. I'm assuming you're already born again and are a branch on the Vine. The next step is self-examination.

6

Step One: Spiritual Examination

Examine yourselves as to whether you are in the faith. Test yourselves.
–2 Cor. 13:5

What reply will you make in that day when at the twinkling of an eye an account is demanded of you for all the time that has been dealt out to you? How have you spent it? –Anselm

Jesus warned us to count the cost of walking with Him: "Whoever does not bear his cross and come after Me cannot be My disciple. For which of you, intending to build a tower, does not sit down first and count the cost, whether he has enough to finish it—lest, after he has laid the foundation, and is not able to finish, all who see it begin to mock him, saying, 'This man began to build and was not able to finish.' Or what king, going to make war against another king, does not sit down first and consider whether he is able with ten thousand to meet him who comes against him with twenty thousand? Or else, while the other is still a great way off, he sends a delegation and asks conditions of peace. So likewise, whoever of you does not forsake all that he has cannot be My disciple" (Luke 14:27-33).

If we're serious about living the fully surrendered Kingdom Life, then we're about to embark on building a great tower to Christ's glory. We're about to plunge into a fierce war against Satan, the world, and our own flesh. Ideally, we counted the costs of discipleship before we were converted and baptized. However, in today's spiritual climate, the emphasis is not on "count the cost." Instead, we're merely invited to ask Jesus to come into our hearts.

When we're ready to embark on the fully surrendered Kingdom Life, the first step we need to take is to examine ourselves. I'm not talking about a quick, cursory scan of our weaknesses. I'm talking about a thorough, no-holds-barred dissection of the state of our souls.

The Dreaded P-Trap

I'm not much of a handyman, but one of the maintenance jobs I handle is fixing our bathroom sinks when they start to drain slowly. Because we're on a septic system, I can't simply pour one of the harsh commercial products down the drain to eat through the stoppage. I know one of the quickest ways to take care of the blockage is to remove the P-trap under the sink and clean out what's there. Yet because I dread the nasty stuff I'm going to find, I invariably try every other possible remedy. I'll put baking soda and vinegar down the drain. If that doesn't work, I'll pour boiling water down it. Anything but removing the P-trap!

However, at some point I usually have to put a bucket under the sink and undo the P-trap. Yuck! Somehow innocent things like soap, toothpaste, and hair turn into horrible gray gunk when they get stuck in the drain. Sometimes just removing and emptying the P-trap isn't enough. I have to push a bent hanger or dowel rod up the drain pipe and bring down whatever goo is still in the pipe. More yuck! Am I ever glad when the disgusting job is over!

That's the kind of spiritual self-examination I'm talking about. Not a simple baking-soda-and-vinegar checkup. Rather, we need to remove the P-traps of our souls and take a look at the horrid gunk that has built up over the years: all the selfishness, envy, greed, vanity, ambition, lust, hatred, anger, prejudice, dishonesty, unforgiveness, complaining, self-pity, bitterness, and pride that reside there. We also need to scrutinize our memory banks to recall all the times we've disobeyed God's commandments and all the times we've hurt and wronged others.

We still aren't finished with our self-scrutiny. What about the fruits of the Christian life? How has our fruit production been? When we look inside ourselves and examine our behavior, do we find "love, joy, peace, longsuffering, kindness, goodness, faithfulness, gentleness, and self-control" (Gal. 5:22-23)? In which of these fruits are we deficient? In which are we strong?

Before we reinstall the P-traps of our souls, we must let others help us in our examination. If we're married, we should ask our spouse for insights into the weaknesses in our lives. What areas do they see that we have not yet surrendered to Christ? What changes do they think we will need to make to be fully surrendered? We should also receive input from mature Christian friends and our church leaders. They will likely see things that we don't.

Let the Bible Help You

There's still one last step in our examination before we can reinstall the P-traps of our souls. No self-examination is complete until we've held up our lives to the light of God's Word. So we should now carefully read through the entire New Testament. Even if we've already read the entire New Testament many times through, this time we will be reading it with a different purpose in mind: To learn everything we can about the Kingdom Life and compare it to our own lives. What does the Kingdom Life look like? Jesus lived a perfect Kingdom Life. What are things we see in His life that are lacking in ours? What commands and exhortations does the New Testament give about the Christian life? What promises does God make to help us live the Kingdom Life? As we carefully read through the New Testament, we may want to highlight all such passages. Or if it's not practical to highlight them, we can keep a notebook at hand on which to list these passages.

When we're finished reading through the New Testament, we should then re-examine our lives in light of all the passages we've read. We may now realize that we need to surrender far more areas of our lives than we originally thought. We may find that there are a lot of sins and ungodly traits that need to be cleaned out.

Our Attitude Toward Sin

Something else we need to examine is our attitude toward sin. God absolutely detests sin (but not the sinner). William Law points out, "Insofar as he sins, every sinner is a friend of the devil's and is carrying on the devil's work against God."[11] Yet some Christians are attracted to sin and even find it amusing or entertaining. Many Christians enjoy novels, movies, and television shows that focus on sin or that present sin in an attractive light. They may laugh at vulgar jokes. What about us?

When Jesus addressed the church in Ephesus in Revelation, He charged them with having lost their first love. Yet even *they* hated the sexual immorality of the Nicolaitans. "This you have, that you hate the deeds of the Nicolaitans, which I also hate" (Rev. 2:6). We hardly hate sexual immorality if we find it entertaining or humorous.

The authentic Kingdom Life leads a person to focus on godliness instead of worldliness. As Paul said, "Whatever things are true, whatever things are noble, whatever things are just, whatever things are pure, whatever things are lovely, whatever things are of good report, if there is any virtue and if there is anything praiseworthy—meditate on these things" (Phil. 4:8). What things do we meditate on or think about? Are they pure, praiseworthy things or are they impure, unworthy things?

What Have We Found?

We've now concluded our self-examination. If we've been brutally honest with ourselves, the picture probably isn't pretty. We've no doubt discovered lots of horrendous, sinful gunk deep inside us. Nineteenth-century preacher Samuel Logan Brengle says this about self-examination:

> The Christian will find a big, dark something in him that wants to get mad when things are against him. Something which will not be patient. Something that is touchy and sensitive. Something that wants to grumble and find fault. Something that is proud and shuns the shame of the Cross. Something that sometimes suggests hard thoughts against God. Something that is self-willed and ugly and sinful.
>
> What is the name of this troublesome "something"? Paul calls it by several names. In the eighth chapter of Romans, he calls it the "carnal mind." In the seventh chapter of Romans, he calls it "the body of this death" and wonders how he can get deliverance from it. In Ephesians and Colossians, he calls it "the old man." In Galatians, he calls it "the flesh." Whatever you wish to call it, it is something evil and awful that remains in the heart after a man has been converted. Rom. 8:7; 7:24; Eph. 4:22; Col. 3:9; Gal. 5:17[12]

Taking Stock for the Quest Ahead

Satan will want to discourage you at this point. "Look at your long list of sins, flaws, and failings," he'll tell you. "You're definitely not cut out for the Kingdom Life." Like Jesus, simply tell him, "Away with you, Satan!" (Matt. 4:10). What's important is not the size or severity of the list, but the size and depth of our faith and love. Christ's power can overcome whatever flaws and sins we have. On our own strength, we would be doomed to wallow in this cesspool of ungodly muck for the rest of our lives. However, we can lift our heads high, for we know that through Christ's power we can overcome whatever sins and weaknesses we have. With His help, we can complete the tower Jesus talked about. With His help we can vanquish our enemies in the spiritual battles ahead.

So don't give in to discouragement, but do ask yourself the following questions:

- To fully live the Kingdom Life, what things need to change in my life?
- What sacrifices will I need to make?
- What areas in my life are presently not surrendered to Christ?
- What are some of the sins that seem to easily entangle me?
- What character flaws have I found in my heart?
- What godly fruit am I producing in my life right now? Where am I deficient?

It might be wise to make a written list of these areas of sin and weakness and of the changes you will need to make with God's help. Then every morning pray for strength to meet those particular challenges, to overcome those particular weaknesses, and to be able to produce the fruit that you're still lacking.

That's one of the reasons we've done this spiritual examination. But there's a second reason.

7

Step Two: Repentance

It is certain we do enough every day to bring us upon our knees at night. –Matthew Henry

Not one day has passed but I have sinned before God. Was this a fitting return for all my Creator's gifts, for my Redeemer's Blood? –Francis of Sales

The individual who truly repents, not only sees sin to be detestable and vile, and worthy of abhorrence, but he really abhors it and hates it in his heart. –Charles Finney

The second reason for our spiritual examination is to bring us to repentance. That's because to a large degree, we can only seriously repent to the extent that we know what we're repenting of.

Deep repentance is another secret of the Kingdom Life. Jesus created an enduring link between repentance and the kingdom of God by making them the joint theme of His gospel: "From that time Jesus began to preach and to say, 'Repent, for the kingdom of heaven is at hand' " (Matt. 4:17).

Repentance Used to Be the Norm

In New Testament times, prospective converts were called upon to thoroughly repent *before* their conversion and baptism. Even John the Baptist required this: "Then Jerusalem, all Judea, and all the region around the Jordan went out to him and were baptized by him in the Jordan, confessing their sins. But when he saw many of the Pharisees and Sadducees coming to his baptism, he said to them, 'Brood of vipers! Who warned you to flee from the wrath to come? Therefore bear fruits worthy of repentance' " (Matt. 3:5-8). So John the Baptist required real repentance before he would baptize anyone. He wanted people to be ready to change their entire way of life because the kingdom of God was at hand. People confessed their sins at the time of baptism. John warned them their lives must continue to bear the fruits of this repentance.

Did things change with the Christian gospel? No. The meaning of baptism changed, but not the requirement to truly repent. The apostles preached to the crowds, "Repent therefore and be converted, that your sins may be blotted out, so that times of refreshing may come from the presence of the Lord" (Acts 3:19). Paul told King Agrippa that he had "declared first to those in Damascus and in Jerusalem, and throughout all the region of Judea, and then to the Gentiles, that they should repent, turn to God, and do works befitting repentance" (Acts 26:20).

Writing about AD 150, Justin Martyr describes baptism in his day: "As many as are persuaded and believe that what we teach and say is true, and undertake to be able to live accordingly, are instructed to pray and to entreat God with fasting for the remission of their past sins. The rest of us pray and fast with them."[13]

The ancient exhortation to repent and confess one's sins before baptism has been replaced today by the anemic invitation merely to "acknowledge that you are a sinner." As a result, millions of people have come to conversion and baptism without ever having confessed and repented of their particular sins. They've only made a general acknowledgement that they are sinners along with the rest of mankind. That is why I recommend combing your mind's memory banks to recall the sins you've committed during your life up to this point. I'm not referring to sins you've already confessed, repented of, and been forgiven. Those are buried and forgotten. I am talking about serious sins that you've never confessed to God and never specifically repented of.

You'll no doubt be able to recollect only a small percentage of your actual sins. But it's likely that the ones you remember will be among your more serious. If you haven't previously repented of these, confess them now to the Lord and repent of them. Likewise, confess and repent of each aspect of the ungodly morass you've discovered inside yourself. The same goes for the fruits of the Spirit that you realize are deficient in your life. As for the many sins, wrongs, faults, and mistakes you've made that you can no longer remember, pray daily, "Forgive us our debts, as we forgive our debtors" (Matt. 6:12).

The Big Surrender

All of this examination, reflection, and repentance is designed to bring you to a point of making a deliberate, total surrender to God. There can be no authentic Kingdom Life without such a surrender. That's why I sometimes refer to those who embark on the Kingdom Life as surrendered Christians.

Anabaptist minister Ken Miller describes this initial, thorough surrender in these words: "This other kind of repentance is the total capitulation of our lives to Jesus at the beginning of the kingdom life. It isn't just repenting of latent character flaws and leftover sinful patterns. It's the total giving up of self. It's where a person turns from serving himself and the kingdoms of this world to decisively surrendering himself to Christ and His kingdom. Such a person has been conquered by the love of God in Christ, and he is ready to sit at the table and sign the terms of surrender."

8

Step Three: Riding the Victorious Cycle

It is the right disposition of the heart towards God that leads people to outward acts of prayer. And on the other side, it is outward acts of prayer that preserve and strengthen the right disposition of the heart towards God. –William Law

The Victorious Cycle is closely connected with producing kingdom fruit. With reference to such fruit, Jesus has told us that without Him we can do nothing (John 15:5). In fact, without His help we would not have been able to make a proper examination of ourselves and to have come to real repentance. But how do we tap into His power to be able to produce fruit? Jesus mentions two things that we have to do: pray and obey.

Jesus invites us, "Ask, and it will be given to you; seek, and you will find; knock, and it will be opened to you. For everyone who asks receives, and he who seeks finds, and to him who knocks it will be opened. Or what man is there among you who, if his son asks for bread, will give him a stone? Or if he asks for a fish, will he give him a serpent? If you then, being evil, know how to give good gifts to your children, how much more will your Father who is in heaven give good things to those who ask Him!" (Matt. 7:7-11). So to receive we must ask—which we do through prayer.

Millions of people pray to God for the power to live the Christian life. But many of them never receive the power they hope for. That's because they don't meet the second condition Jesus gives: "If you love Me, keep My commandments. And I will pray the Father, and He will give you another Helper, that He may abide with you forever. . . . If you keep My commandments, you will abide in My love, just as I have kept My Father's commandments and abide in His love" (John 14:15,16; 15:10).

Although prayer is the primary channel to bring in God's power to live the Christian life, we need to be living the Christian life for our prayers to be effective. As James said, "The effective, fervent prayer of a *righteous* man avails much" (Jas. 5:16). What about the fervent prayer of an unrighteous man? Apparently it avails little.

Peter makes this point clear in his first epistle: "The eyes of the Lord are on the righteous, and His ears are open to their prayers. But the face of the Lord is against those who do evil" (1 Pet. 3:12). So God hears the prayers of the righteous, but He turns away from the wicked. Accordingly, our obedience makes a significant difference as to whether our prayers are answered.

Peter also points out the purifying effect obedience has on our souls. He writes, "You have purified your souls in obeying the truth through the Spirit" (1 Pet. 1:22). In this passage, Peter isn't talking about our initial conversion or new birth. Rather, he is addressing those of us who are born-again Christians. He tells us that obeying the truth has a purifying effect on our souls.

Riding a Bike

The Victorious Cycle is a lot like riding a bike. To be able to ride a bike, you must be able to keep your balance. But it's almost impossible to balance yourself on a bike unless it's moving. So you have to be balanced to move; yet you have to be moving to keep your balance. At first, this sounds like a catch-22, but it's not. Most of us have learned to ride bikes. You move a little, and that helps you get your balance. Your balance then helps you to move a bit more. That helps you balance even more, enabling you to move that much faster . . . and before you know it, you're riding a bike. It sounds complicated, but as most of us have experienced, once we get the knack of riding a bicycle, it's something we can do without thinking.

The Kingdom Life is very similar. To live an obedient life, we need power from God. To have power from God, we must pray. However, for our prayers to be effective, we must be living an obedient life. Once again, it sounds like a catch-22, but it's not. In fact, learning to walk with God is as easy as learning to ride a bike. We pray for power to live an obedient life in a particular area. Then we step out in faith, deny our flesh, and obey that particular commandment.

Yes, it is difficult at first. However, this initial obedience enhances our prayer life. So the next time we pray, our prayers avail more than they did previously. So now our prayers provide us with even more power to obey. As we continue to obey, our prayers become even more effective. This in turn gives us even more power to obey. We now can step out in faith to obey other commands that we've previously neglected. This, in turn, causes our prayers to avail that much more, giving us additional power to obey. And so on.

It's what I call the Victorious Cycle. It works like a vicious cycle, except that it operates in reverse. My dictionary defines a vicious cycle as "a situation in which an attempt to resolve one problem creates new problems that lead back to the original situation."[14] For example, parents in a developing country may be struggling to provide food, clothing, and housing for their family. So they take their children out of school and put them to work. The income from the children helps the family to survive. However, without an education, their children are doomed to low-paying jobs as adults. As a result, these adult children struggle to support their own families. So they too take their children out of school to help provide for the family. And the cycle goes on.

The Victorious Cycle works similarly, except that it's something good, and it's something very powerful.

The Great Secret of the Kingdom Life

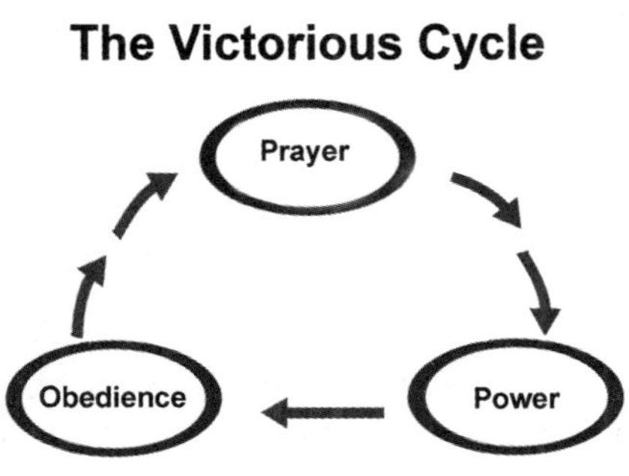

The Victorious Cycle is one of the great secrets of the Kingdom Life that so many Christians miss. Too many Christians think they can simply add prayer to an otherwise ungodly, pleasure-driven life and that God is then going to do all of the work for them. It has never worked that way, and it never will.

Concerning the need for prayer and obedience to work together, the anonymous author of *The Kneeling Christian* writes: "This truth is so clearly taught in Scripture that it is amazing that any should try to retain both sin and prayer. Yet very many do this. David cried long ages ago, 'If I regard iniquity in my heart, the Lord will not hear' (Psalms 66:18). And Isaiah says, 'Your iniquities have separated between you and your God, and your sins have hid his face from you' " (Isaiah 59:2).[15]

William Law minces no words in declaring that prayer accompanied by disobedience will get us nowhere:

> Bended knees, while you are clothed with pride? Heavenly petitions, while you are hoarding up treasures upon earth? Holy devotions, while you live in the follies of the world? Prayers of meekness and charity, while your heart is the seat of pride and resentment? Spending *hours* of prayer, while you give up *years* to idle amusements, impertinent visits, and foolish pleasures? These are all absurd and unacceptable services to God. It's like words of thanksgiving coming from a person who lives in discontent.
>
> Unless the common course of our lives is according to the common spirit of our prayers, our prayers are far from being a real or sufficient degree of devotion. They are nothing but lip-service—or, what is worse—flagrant hypocrisy.[16]

Adding Faith

To make our illustration simple, I've only mentioned two factors: prayer and obedience. But now let's add a third element to strengthen our Victorious Cycle. That element is faith. Jesus explains, "If you have faith and do not doubt, you shall not only do what was done to the fig tree, but even if you say to this mountain, 'Be taken up and cast into the sea,' it shall happen. And all things you ask in prayer, believing, you will receive" (Matt. 21:21-22).

So for our prayers to be particularly effective we need not only obedience, but also faith. When we ask in faith, our prayers are much more apt to be answered. This, in turn, gives us more power to obey God. As we see God's transforming power in our lives, this strengthens our faith further. With stronger faith, our prayers are that much more effective. And so on.

So how can we develop a regular prayer life?

OUR PRAYER AND DEVOTIONAL LIFE

9

Developing a Strong Prayer Life

What a shame is this to us, that God is more willing to be prayed to, and more ready to hear prayer than we are to pray. –Matthew Henry

What is the reason that some believers are so much brighter and more godly than others? I believe the difference, in nineteen cases out of twenty, arises from different habits of private prayer. –J. C. Ryle

William Law observed, "Prayer is the nearest approach to God and the highest enjoyment of God of which we are capable in this life."[17] Yet the average Christian spends less than ten minutes a day in prayer. I'm not speaking about nominal, inactive Christians. I'm talking about active, church-going Christians. Are we among them?

Since so many Christians find prayer difficult, why does God require it? The reason goes back to God's purpose in creating angels and humans in the first place. He loves having children for the same reason we do: we cherish our relationship with them. There is little joy in being a parent if we have no meaningful rapport with our children. It's the ongoing loving relationship between parent and child that brings joy. That's why God walked with Adam and Eve in the Garden. He loved interacting with them, and He loves interacting with us today.

"But God Already Knows My Needs"

"Yes," you may object, "but the reason I talk with my parents is to keep them up-to-date with what's going on in my life. Also I want to communicate my needs to them and express my gratitude for things they've done. But God already knows all those things before I even open my mouth. So what's the point of telling Him?"

It's true that God already knows all things before we tell Him, but He still wants to hear about them from *us*. When my children were little, they typically engaged in fun activities with my wife Deborah while I was away at work or in school. When I got home, Deborah usually filled me in on everything she had done with the children that day.

So did that mean I didn't ask the children what they had done? Not at all. I still asked them what they did that day. Why? *Because I wanted to hear it from their own lips*. It brought me enormous pleasure to hear *them* tell it to me themselves. I wanted to see the joy on their faces or their concerned looks. I wanted to be able to interact with them personally, even though I already knew all about their day.

It's the same way with God. He wants to hear you and me tell Him what's happening in our lives. He already knows our needs, but He wants to hear us express those needs. He wants to know that we're depending upon Him, rather than taking Him for granted. He already knows whether or not we're thankful for the things we receive from Him, but He still wants to hear us express it. If I give my children gifts, I know they're thankful without their having to say it. But it still means a lot to me to receive a thank-you card from them.

It's hard to have much of a relationship without communication. With every beam of sunshine, every drop of rain on the thirsty ground, and every page of the Bible we read, God is telling us how much He loves us. And He wants to hear personally from us how much we love Him.

Prayer Is Not Meant to Be a Burden

God never intended prayer to be a burden. As William Law noted, "When our hearts are full of God, sending up holy desires to the throne of grace, we are then in our highest state, we are upon the utmost heights of human greatness. We are not before kings and princes, but in the presence and audience of the Lord of all the world. We can be no higher until death is swallowed up in glory."[18]

If you find that prayer is more of a burden to you than a joy, don't despair. Like so many other things in the Christian life, God will help bring you to a point where you will find prayer a delight instead of a duty. However, you have to start where you are. Get on the Victorious Cycle and ride it. Pray regularly and often, even if at present you do so only out of duty. The mere act of praying regularly will help you reach the point where prayer becomes a delight. As God changes your heart in so many other matters, He will change it toward prayer as well.

Special Times of Prayer

When should you pray? Anytime and everywhere. Yet that doesn't mean that you shouldn't schedule regular times of prayer. In biblical times, God's people had regular set times of prayer throughout the day. Today the average active Christian prays only before meals. If he is more serious than average, he also prays when he gets up and before he goes to bed. But that's about it.

That used to describe my prayer life as well. So I was quite surprised when I first read the early Christian writings and discovered they had more regularly scheduled times of prayer than that. For one thing, they always prayed both *before* and *after* meals. They all also prayed at the third, the sixth, and the ninth hours—that is, at 9:00 a.m., 12:00 noon, and 3:00 p.m.[19] At first I thought these prayer times were some sort of manmade custom invented by the early Christians. But later, when I was reading the Scriptures, I realized that the apostles and prophets had similar prayer times.

For example, did you ever notice that Daniel had three set times of prayer each day? Even when Persian law forbade prayer to the true God, the Scriptures say this about Daniel: "Now when Daniel knew that the writing was signed, he went home. And in his upper room, with his windows open toward Jerusalem, he knelt down on his knees three times that day, and prayed and gave thanks before his God, *as was his custom since early days*" (Dan. 6:10).

Daniel's prayer times were evidently more than his personal custom. Daniel no doubt prayed at the third, sixth, and ninth hours—the special hours of prayer for both the Jews and the early Christians. We read in Acts, "Now Peter and John went up together to the temple at the hour of prayer, the ninth hour." So the ninth hour was not just the apostles' special hour of prayer, but that of the Jews as well. Again we read in Acts that Cornelius "gave alms generously to the people, and prayed to God always. About the ninth hour of the day he saw clearly in a vision an angel of God." And still again, "The next day, as they went on their journey and drew near the city, Peter went up on the housetop to pray, about the sixth hour" (Acts 3:1; 10:2,3,9).

Of course, maintaining these prayer hours is not a commandment from God. Yet the discipline of keeping regular times of prayer throughout the day is one of the secrets to living the Kingdom Life. It's been one of the great losses of the church that so few Christians keep these ancient prayer times. Imagine the power the New Testament church experienced when the entire church prayed together at these hours of the day. Picture the sense of unity individual Christians felt in knowing that when they knelt to pray at these special times, the entire church was praying with them.

Whether or not you're ready to work these ancient prayer times into your daily schedule at present, there are two times each day (in addition to meals) that no Christian should neglect to pray: morning and night.

Early Morning Prayer

Seventeenth-century Welsh minister Matthew Henry wrote, "Morning is the first part of the day. And it is fitting that He who is the First should have the first and be served the first."[20]

What should we pray about each morning? Virtually everything is fitting. Have you had a peaceful and restful night's sleep? Thank God for it. Did anxieties or ailments keep you from sleeping well? If so, pray about those anxieties or ailments. What sins seem to easily entangle you on most days? Pray that God will enable you to be victorious over them today. Is there a family member, neighbor, or co-worker with whom you often clash? Pray that God will help you say and do the right things today concerning that person.

It's fitting to pray the Lord's Prayer along with our other early morning petitions, for in it we ask, "Give us this day our daily bread." Then there are our work and family responsibilities. Surely we want to ask for God's guidance and blessings on these. During morning prayer, we should entrust our families and loved ones into God's care.

We also need God's guidance and strength to help us with any unexpected events that may arise during the day. And we should pray about the problems we face on a daily basis. We not only need strength and wisdom to meet these, but to handle them in a godly manner. In fact, we need to commit each day to God's service, so that we can be a help and blessing to all those with whom we interact.

Perhaps you have a list of people to intercede for. Morning is a good time to make such intercessions. Jesus said that we are to seek first the Kingdom. Make it your morning prayer that you will put Kingdom interests first throughout the day.

The list is almost endless. There is so much to pray for in the morning that many committed Christians schedule their daily devotional hour in the morning. We'll be talking more about the devotional hour in the next chapter. However, if it does not work for you to set aside an extended time for morning prayer, then you can pray about all of these topics while dressing, showering, commuting, or doing other mundane tasks.

10

Nightly Examination

Another important secret to living the Kingdom Life is nightly examination and repentance. I schedule my devotional hour at night, so I make this examination part of my devotional time. If your devotional time is in the morning, then make this nightly examination a part of your bedtime prayers.

Ironically, I have come to love this nightly examination and repentance. At first I thought I must be odd in this respect. So I was encouraged when I came across the following statement from Henry Scougal, "Repentance itself is a delightful exercise when it flows from love."[21] Why would a surrendered Christian find examination and repentance delightful? Because if we've had a victorious day, it is extremely encouraging to review the day's events with God and lay before Him those victories. If we've had a day of sin and failure, it's like laying down a heavy burden to confess these transgressions and failures to God and seek His forgiveness. So either way, nightly examination and repentance is something we should look forward to.

The following is my particular method of examination. You may find it helpful as a model. First, while in prayer before God, I think back to the very beginning of that day's events, when I woke up that morning. From there I go chronologically through the day's events one by one. If I overcame a temptation or handled a situation in a godly manner, I thank God for giving me the victory.

When I come to areas of failures or wrong attitudes, I confess and repent of them. But more than that I analyze what the particular circumstances were that led to those failings. I've found that my daily failings typically come when I'm responding to other people's actions or to unexpected negative events. As a result, I'm learning to be particularly vigilant at such times, for that is when I'm most likely to sin. In addition to confessing and repenting, I also ask God to give me victory the next time I'm faced with a similar test.

When I speak of repentance, I'm referring to something more than a quick "I'm sorry." Genuine repentance means to have profound remorse for sin. It means to feel deep sorrow and regret for rebelling against God. Those living the Kingdom Life don't just admit to general wrongdoing, but they also acknowledge that they've committed crimes against God Himself. William Law writes, "A confession that is without this sorrow and compunction of heart has nothing in it either to make amends for past sins or to produce in us any true reform and amendment of life."[22] Part of making amends is to apologize to any persons we may have hurt, and ask for their forgiveness.

The benefits from such nightly examination are threefold:

- It enables us to confess and repent of particular sins, not just sins in general.

- It makes us that much more aware of our conduct throughout each day, knowing we're going to be giving an account to God at the end of the day.

- Having gone to bed with a fresh recollection of that day's failings, they should still be fresh on our minds the next morning. So the next morning we can prepare our armor and weapons to vanquish those foes if they arise.

Although I've emphasized our sins and failings, it's good to mull over *all* of the day's activities with God—the victories and incidentals, as well as the failures. Go through the events of the day one by one and talk to God about them. Don't worry that you are leaving God waiting as you mentally peruse the day's events. He has endless patience and endless time. You never have to worry that He will hang up on you. By reviewing the day with God, you can receive His help in remembering its events. He delights in your conversing with Him in this way, just as a mother would delight in sitting down with her child and hearing her child talk about that day's events.

If you've followed the suggestions in this chapter, you're on your way to a strong prayer life. But there is still another decisive step you need to take.

11

Establishing Your Devotional Hour

We first make our habits; and then our habits make us. –John Dryden

All ways of life that tend to nourish, raise, and fix our affections upon Him are to be reckoned as so many helps and means to fill us with devotion. –William Law

When we read the biographies of spiritual giants, we find that almost without exception they steadfastly maintained a daily devotional hour. So one of the most important secrets to living the Kingdom Life is to establish such an hour. In fact, I can almost say without exception that without such a devotional hour, you won't go very far in the Kingdom Life. Incidentally, when I say "devotional hour," I don't mean that it has to be a full sixty minutes. Eventually you'll probably *want* to spend a full hour, but there's nothing magical about sixty minutes.

In the next few chapters, we'll be talking about how to make your devotional time a rich spiritual experience. In our discussion, I will address matters as though you are alone during this devotional time. This is because we all need some personal, one-on-one time with God. Nevertheless, if you are married, you will no doubt want to do some of these things with your spouse and with your children.

When Should You Schedule Your Devotional Hour?

Most people will find that the best time for their devotional hour is first thing in the morning. David wrote, "O God, You are my God; early will I seek You" (Ps. 63:1). Job rose early each morning to offer sacrifices for his children. Under the Law, the priests offered up a lamb every morning, and the high priest burned incense on the altar (Exod. 29:39; 30:7). We read concerning Jesus, "Now in the morning, having risen a long while before daylight, He went out and departed to a solitary place; and there He prayed" (Mark 1:35).

Many people find that their minds are freshest in the morning and their hearts are the most undistracted at that time. Starting the day with a regular prayer time is one way to keep Christ and His Kingdom foremost in our lives throughout the day. Andrew Murray wrote, "The Kingdom should be first every day and all the day. Let the Kingdom be first every morning. Begin the day with God, and God Himself will maintain His Kingdom in your heart."[23]

However, some may find that morning is not the best time for their devotional hour. Instead of being the freshest in the morning, your head may be full of cobwebs. Perhaps morning is the most harried time in your home. If you're a mother, you may be busy getting the family dressed and fed and getting your children off to school or ready for homeschool. If you're a man, you may be rushing off to work. Some would suggest that you should simply get up earlier so you can have your prayer time before all the commotion starts. Perhaps so. But getting up earlier may only cause you to go through the day extra tired.

For years I tried to develop a regular devotional hour each morning. I scheduled it in the morning because almost all devotional books insist that one's devotional hour should be the first thing each day. But I'm not a morning person; I'm a night owl. I do my best thinking, my best writing, and my best praying at night. Nevertheless, for years I tried to force myself into the morning devotional hour mold.

One day I finally realized that the Scriptures nowhere command us to have a *morning* devotional hour. In fact, they don't require us to have a devotional hour at all. The devotional hour is simply an important aid to living the Kingdom Life. So I was unnecessarily forcing myself into a mold that didn't fit me. I eventually realized that I needed my devotional hour to fit *my* life and not someone else's. When I moved my devotional hour from morning to evening, it changed from being a dutiful chore to being a joy.

To be sure, you should always begin your day with prayer. But it can be a shorter prayer time. You can then reserve a different part of the day for your devotional hour. Choose the time of day that best fits you. Some people may find the best time for them is during their lunch break. If you're a mother with small children, you may find your best devotional time is in the afternoon when the children are taking naps.

The important thing is to find a time when you will not feel rushed and when you are unlikely to be interrupted. Schedule your devotional hour for a time when you can clear your mind of the cares of the day and truly focus on God.

Does It Need to Be an Hour?

As I said earlier, there is nothing magical about sixty minutes. In fact, if your devotional life has been spotty or nonexistent, I don't advise you to suddenly start praying and reading for an hour each day. If you try a lengthy devotional time before you're ready, it will almost certainly be a drudgery. Instead, start with a five-minute special prayer time, followed by five minutes of Bible reading.

Once you have established this devotional time each day, examine the *quality* of your prayer during this time. Is your prayer time dry and mechanical? Do you have difficulty filling up the five minutes? Are you mainly praying out of a sense of duty? Would you rather be doing something else? If the answer to any of these questions is yes, then there's no point in making your prayer time any longer. Instead, focus on improving the quality of your five-minute prayer time. Ask God to help kindle a desire in you to pray.

If you persevere, eventually you will find that you have no trouble filling the five minutes with meaningful prayer. In fact, you will come to love this five minutes with God and will look forward to it each day. When you have reached that point and are consistent with it, then increase your prayer time to ten minutes, followed by five or ten minutes of Bible reading. Ask yourself the same questions about your ten-minute prayer time. When you find that your ten minutes of prayer are fruitful and something you cherish, try increasing the time to fifteen minutes, and so on.

Finally, there is nothing that limits your devotional time to one hour. In fact, you might want to begin the day with a devotional hour and end it in the same manner.

Where Should I Pray?

Jesus said, "When you pray, go into your room, and when you have shut your door, pray to your Father who is in the secret place; and your Father who sees in secret will reward you openly" (Matt. 6:6). The word *secret* here doesn't mean that no one else can know where it is. It means secluded or hidden away.

Jesus not only gave us the command to pray in secret, but He also set the example. He often sought quiet places of solitude to pray. Before He began His ministry, He spent forty days alone in the wilderness praying and fasting (Matt. 4:1-2). He spent an entire night alone praying on a mountain before selecting His twelve apostles (Luke 6:12-13). Both after John the Baptists' death and after feeding the five thousand, He withdrew to solitary places (Matt. 14:13,23). In preparation for his arrest and crucifixion, He sought the solitude of the Garden of Gethsemane to pray. It's true that He had His eleven faithful apostles with Him in the garden, but He withdrew a distance even from them in order to have complete solitude for His prayers (Matt. 26:36-46).

So find a solitary place for your devotional hour. The ideal is to have a room, or corner of a room, set aside in your home or business for this very purpose. William Law makes this suggestion:

> As far as you can, always pray in the same place. If you are to reserve that place for devotion, and not allow yourself to do anything commonplace in it; if you are never to be there yourself, but in times of devotion. If any little room, or (if that cannot be) if any particular part of a room were thus used, this kind of consecration of it as a place holy unto God, will have an effect upon your mind and dispose you to such a mental state as will very much assist your devotion.
>
> For by having a place thus sacred in your room, it would in some measure resemble a chapel or house of God. This would dispose you to be always in the spirit of Christianity when you were there; and fill you with wise and holy thoughts when you were by yourself there.[24]

Of course, you may not be able to set aside such a place. Don't let that trouble you. Jesus had no place to call home, and so He had no one special place of prayer. He had to seek out a solitary place wherever He happened to be. Finally, if you have no choice but to pray in public, then do so—just don't do it to be seen by others. When Paul and Silas were in jail in Philippi, they had no choice but to pray and sing publicly in the presence of the other prisoners. The Scriptures say, "At midnight Paul and Silas were praying and singing hymns to God, and the prisoners were listening to them" (Acts 16:25).

Up to this point we've talked about when and where to pray, but *what* should we pray about?

12

Enriching Your Devotions

He that goes to his closet in a hurry, only to repeat a short form of words, may pray all his life without any real devotion. – William Law

There are certain means of assisting our devotion, some rules, though little in themselves, yet of great use to render our minds attentive and fervent in our supplications to God. –William Law

The reason I use the term "devotional hour" instead of "prayer hour" is that you'll be spending this time in prayer, reflection, Bible reading, devotional reading, and perhaps singing and worship. Depending upon your circumstances and your ability to pray, you may do more reading and reflecting than praying. That's up to you. Obviously, don't get so engaged in your reading that you neglect praying.

I want to share some suggestions for a fruitful, meaningful devotional hour. If you already have a successful format, there's no need to change it. These suggestions are mainly for those who don't already have a daily devotional time. Use them if they're helpful; ignore them if they're not.

Entering His Presence

After you have gone into your prayer room and shut the door, it's good to consciously enter the Lord's presence. You may want to visualize coming before God's majestic throne. You may find it helpful to think of the picture that Isaiah gives of God enthroned with his angels: "I saw the Lord sitting on a throne, high and lifted up, and the train of His robe filled the temple. Above it stood seraphim; each one had six wings: with two he covered his face, with two he covered his feet, and with two he flew. And one cried to another and said: 'Holy, holy, holy is the Lord of hosts; The whole earth is full of His glory!' " (Isa. 6:1-3).

Or perhaps you will want to imagine that you are blind and have just been brought before a majestic king sitting on his throne. You can't see him, but you are fully aware of his presence. It's the same when you come before the throne of heaven—only infinitely greater.

Or, instead of focusing on God's majesty, you may find it more helpful to concentrate on God's love and His kindness. In that case, you might want to envision the loving father in Jesus' parable of the prodigal son. Picture yourself at the knees of this loving Father, pouring out your heart to Him. And this is entirely appropriate, for God is not far off. In fact, He is closer to your soul than your own flesh is. He is literally right beside you when you pray.

Regardless of how you wish to picture God—or if you prefer not to picture Him at all—spend a minute or two just enjoying His presence. Use this time to free your mind of all distracting thoughts so you can focus on God alone. Think about the greatness of the Person you're about to address. Think about His love and His eagerness to hear your prayers. What a privilege it is to be able to talk to Him.

What Is the Appropriate Posture During Prayer?

The Bible does not command us to use any particular posture when praying, although it does direct us to "lift up holy hands" when we pray (1 Tim. 2:8). The best posture is the one that is most natural to you and that enhances a prayerful mood.

For most Western Christians, kneeling is probably the posture we most associate with prayer. This was apparently Daniel's custom, too. The Scriptures tell us that "he knelt down on his knees three times that day" (Dan. 6:10).

The early Christians used different prayer postures depending upon the occasion and upon the nature of their prayers. When praising God or giving thanks, they normally prayed standing with their hands lifted to heaven. Since every Sunday was a celebration of the Resurrection, they prayed standing on Sundays. When supplicating God, they typically prayed kneeling (except on Sundays). When confessing serious sins, they sometimes prayed lying prostrate on the ground. Jesus described the penitent tax collector praying in the following manner: "Standing afar off, he would not so much as raise his eyes to heaven, but beat his breast, saying, 'God be merciful to me a sinner!' " (Luke 18:13).

Jesus also used different postures when praying, depending on the situation. When giving thanks for the loaves and fishes, "He looked up to heaven, blessed and broke the loaves" (Mark 6:41). However, in the Garden of Gethsemane making supplications to His Father, "He knelt down and prayed" (Luke 22:41). At one point in the garden when praying intensely, He "fell on His face and prayed" (Matt. 26:39).

So you may want to change your posture depending upon the nature of your prayers at that particular moment. But what are some of the things we should be praying about?

13

What to Pray About

In the past century or so, many Christians have been taught that it is unspiritual to pray the Lord's Prayer. But Jesus instructed us to pray it. "One of His disciples said to Him, 'Lord, teach us to pray, as John also taught his disciples.' So He said to them, 'When you pray, say: Our Father in heaven . . .' " (Luke 11:1-2).

And again, in the Sermon on the Mount, Jesus said, "In this manner, therefore, pray: Our Father which art in heaven, Hallowed be thy name. Thy kingdom come. Thy will be done in earth, as it is in heaven. Give us this day our daily bread. And forgive us our debts, as we forgive our debtors. And lead us not into temptation, but deliver us from evil: For thine is the kingdom, and the power, and the glory, for ever. Amen" (Matt. 6:9-13, KJV).

There is probably no other prayer we can pray and know beyond a doubt that every word we say is inspired by the Holy Spirit. So the wise and obedient Christian will pray the Lord's Prayer. Notice that I said *pray* the Lord's Prayer. Don't just recite it by rote memory without your heart entering into the prayer. Make every word of it your own. I like to pray this prayer at the beginning of my devotional hour, after coming into God's presence. Others may prefer to close their devotional time with this prayer.

Most of us know this prayer so well that there is the constant danger of not thinking about the words as we're praying them. I find it meaningful to first pray the Lord's

Prayer just as Jesus gave it to us. Then I pray it again, but the second time I paraphrase it and personalize it. For example:

> Our great and most wonderful Father in heaven, may your name be sanctified and glorified everywhere. Help me to live my life today so that my life will hallow and glorify your name. May your kingdom come soon and rule over the entire earth. Father, use me in any way you desire to serve your kingdom. May your will be done everywhere here on earth just as the angels in heaven are doing it. But again, Father, help me to do your will this day in all of my actions and thoughts.
>
> I ask only that you provide for me this day what I truly need to live, and I thank you, Father, that you have provided much more than I actually need. Help me to use this surplus to bless others. Please forgive me my sins as I forgive others. And help me, Father, to be more forgiving, to keep account of no injuries.
>
> Please lead me today away from the path of temptation. I know Satan would like for me to do his will today, not yours. Please protect me from whatever schemes he has in mind for me.

The idea here is not to improve on the Lord's Prayer. We can't do that. Rather, the thought is to paraphrase it and personalize it in such a manner that we have to slow down and think of every word we're saying—and mean it.

Having prayed the Lord's Prayer, we know that we have prayed for the things Christ says are the most important. We are now free to pray about other significant matters. Generally speaking, these other matters fall under one of the following six categories: thanksgiving, praise, intercession, personal needs, personal guidance, and confession.

Thanksgiving and Praise

Thanksgiving should be at the top of our prayer lists. "In everything give thanks; for this is the will of God in Christ Jesus for you" (1 Thess. 5:18). We have so much to be thankful for:

- Life itself
- Our salvation
- Our spouse and family
- God's Word
- Our church, friends, and homes
- Our food, clothing, and necessities of life
- Our employment

That list is, of course, just a start. As we grow in contentment and thankfulness, the list of things to be thankful for keeps growing. In addition to praising God for the personal things He has done for us, we can praise Him for His attributes, His creation, His actions in human history, and what He has planned for the future of the universe.

Intercession

After thanking God, we should intercede on behalf of our family, friends, church family, neighbors, co-workers, and other people with whom we interact. We can pray that God deliver them from certain trials or for victory over temptations and weaknesses. We can also pray for their spiritual and physical health and for particular blessings in their lives. We should also pray for our government leaders, legislators, and judges. "Therefore I exhort first of all that supplications, prayers, intercessions, and giving of thanks be made for all men, for kings and all who are in authority, that we may lead a quiet and peaceable life in all godliness and reverence. For this is good and acceptable in the sight of God our Savior" (1 Tim. 2:1-3).

Paul and the other New Testament Christians interceded for one another on a regular basis. Paul told Timothy, "Without ceasing I remember you in my prayers night and day" (2 Tim. 1:3). How many people do we intercede for in that manner? One reason Paul was so effective as a missionary was because he spent so much time interceding on behalf of the people to whom he ministered. He and Timothy declared to the Colossians, "We give thanks to the God and Father of our Lord Jesus Christ, praying always for you. . . . For this reason we also, since the day we heard it, do not cease to pray for you, and to ask that you may be filled with the knowledge of His will in all wisdom and spiritual understanding; that you may walk worthy of the Lord, fully pleasing Him, being fruitful in every good work and increasing in the knowledge of God" (Col. 1:3,9-10).

Imagine the spiritual health of our congregations if we all prayed for one another's spiritual well-being the way Paul and Timothy prayed for others! But don't wait for others to begin doing it; start praying daily for each family in your congregation. Not only will this bless others, but it will also have an amazing spiritual effect on you. William Law wrote about this aspect of intercession:

> Such intercessions, besides the great love they display, will have a mighty effect upon your own heart. It will dispose you to every other good duty and to the exercise of every other virtue towards such persons that you have so often been praying about. . . . For there is nothing that makes us love a person so much as praying for him. And when you can once do this sincerely for any person, you have fitted your soul for the performance of everything that is kind and civil towards him.[25]

Personal Needs and Guidance

After thanking God and interceding on behalf of others, it's time to pray for ourselves. The order Jesus gave us in the Lord's Prayer is to pray for spiritual matters first and our material needs second. In chapter 10 we talked about the need to examine ourselves. What is the condition of our spiritual health? In what areas of our lives are we spiritually weak? What fruits of the Spirit do we lack? Are we having problems in our marriage, at our jobs, with friends, or with members of our congregation? Has anyone wronged us whom we haven't forgiven? Are we struggling with any sins—such as lust, gossip, impatience, or envy? Do we have a critical spirit? Are we coveting any material things or spiritual positions? We should pray about these matters. We should also pray that God will help us to see sins and weaknesses in ourselves to which we are perhaps blind.

Having prayed first for our spiritual needs, it is now appropriate to pray for our physical needs. Notice how Jesus worded this: "Give us this day our daily bread." He didn't authorize us to pray for tomorrow's bread, let alone to pray for riches and vanities. Jesus also purposefully worded the request in the collective—give *us* our daily bread. So we should not only pray for our own needs, but also for the needs of others. In fact, if we live in the United States or Western Europe, our *needs* have been most likely more than met. We should still pray for our daily bread as Jesus commanded, but we should particularly pray for food and the other necessities of life for those living in underdeveloped countries.

Confession

We should never conclude our devotional hour without confessing our sins. Why? John explains, "If we say that we have no sin, we deceive ourselves, and the truth is not in us. If we confess our sins, He is faithful and just to forgive us our sins and to cleanse us from all unrighteousness. If we say that we have not sinned, we make Him a liar, and His word is not in us" (1 John 1:8-10).

Two things stand out in this passage concerning our prayer life. First, we should never imagine we have no sins to confess. Second, God's promise of forgiveness and cleansing is conditioned on our confessing our sins. Some Christians imagine that all of their future sins were pre-forgiven when they were originally saved. However, the Scriptures make no such promise. In fact, they expressly tell us otherwise. "He who covers his sins will not prosper, but whoever confesses and forsakes them will have mercy" (Prov. 28:13).

Needless to say, confession is meaningless if we're not repentant. If we don't have godly sorrow for our sins, our confession doesn't mean much. Furthermore, Jesus conditions forgiveness of sins on our forgiving others. "If you forgive men their trespasses, your heavenly Father will also forgive you. But if you do not forgive men their trespasses, neither will your Father forgive your trespasses" (Matt. 6:14-15).

Prayer List

You may find it helpful to keep a printed prayer list. This way you won't forget to pray for matters needing your attention. If you use a computer on a regular basis, you might find it useful to keep your prayer list on your computer, where you can easily modify it and print updated versions every day or perhaps every week.

But Christians have been keeping prayer lists and prayer journals for centuries before the computer was ever invented. So you can easily keep a handwritten list, crossing off items that no longer need prayer and adding new items. Don't let your prayer list become stale. When you tell people at church or other places that you will pray for them or for a particular need, be sure to add it to your prayer list right away so you don't forget about it.

What If My Mind Wanders?

If your mind wanders while you pray, take heart—it indicates you're praying long enough for your mind to have time to wander. People who only pray for a minute or two a day don't have that problem. You can also take heart in the fact that nearly every spiritual writer from the Middle Ages through today talks about this problem. This suggests that even these spiritual giants dealt with this problem in their prayer lives.

Remember, it is better to pray and have your mind wander than not to pray at all. So don't let a wandering mind discourage you from praying. God is very patient. At the same time, you should analyze the situation. Where does your mind go? Does it turn to problems that are weighing on you? If so, consciously bring those matters into your prayer. Do you use a prayer list when praying? If not, you may find it helpful. I find that my mind wanders much less when I'm going down a list. Also, add the problem of a wandering mind to your list of things to pray about. God can help you drown out distracting thoughts while you're praying.

I'll share with you another secret to overcoming wandering thoughts: break your prayer time into a series of very short prayers. Once you've completed a thought, close the prayer in Jesus' name and say amen. Then when your mind is refocused, pray another short prayer until you have once again completed an entire thought. Then close that prayer. By praying a series of short prayers, it gives your mind the opportunity to explore other thoughts between these short prayers, instead of your mind wandering in the middle of a long prayer.

Up to this point in our devotional hour, we have been doing most of the talking. It's important now to let God talk to us.

14

Reading the Scriptures and Spiritual Classics

During the time we've been praying, God has no doubt brought various thoughts to our minds and given us guidance. However, interpreting which thoughts have come from God is highly subjective. In contrast, when we read the Bible, we can be certain we're hearing from God. Matthew Henry noted, "The Bible is a letter God has sent to us; prayer is a letter we send to him."[26] So we should set aside part of our devotional hour for God to speak to us through His written Word.

The type of Bible reading we want to do during this time is devotional reading, rather than exegetical Bible study. In devotional reading, we are consciously remaining in God's presence and letting Him speak to us through His Word. In a sense, devotional Bible reading is also interactive reading. Because as we read, we should also be constantly praying—praising God, confessing disobedience in our lives concerning the things we read, making commitments to live by what we're reading, and asking for the power to do so.

Reading the Great Spiritual Classics

I also recommend that you spend a portion of your devotional hour reading some of the great spiritual classics. Of course, we don't read them the same way we read Scripture, for they were written by fallible humans. Nevertheless, many of the great spiritual classics particularly address the Kingdom Life under various names, and they contain useful insights from fellow travelers along this narrow way.

My all-time favorite spiritual classic is William Law's *A Serious Call to a Devout and Holy Life*. For someone wanting to progress toward a fully surrendered life, I can recommend no better book. It was this book that so inspired John Wesley, Charles Wesley, and George Whitefield. It lies at the foundation of both the Great Awakening and the Methodist revivals. In fact, to a large degree, through their preaching, the Wesleys were attempting to bring the spirituality of *A Serious Call* to the masses.

One thing to keep in mind when reading *A Serious Call* is that the author assumes that the reader is already on the Vine. It's not a book to give to an unconverted person. It doesn't really address the need for conversion. And I think it's fair to say that in *A Serious Call*, William Law doesn't put enough emphasis on grace. He does not omit it, but I think he could have emphasized it more. In his later works he writes a lot more about the new birth and the role of grace.

One of the things that makes *A Serious Call* so special is that William Law lived everything he wrote. None of what he says is pious imaginings. It basically describes the life he and his close companions were living. Law wrote many other spiritual books and pamphlets. The following are four of my favorites:

An Earnest Address to the English Clergy

A Treatise on Christian Perfection

Of Justification by Faith and Works—A Dialogue With a Methodist

The Spirit of Prayer

You will also be blessed by the works of many other spiritual writers and teachers. I recommend the following spiritual classics:

The Life of God in the Soul of Man by Henry Scougal
On the Imitation of Christ by Thomas á Kempis
Let Go by Fenelon
The Complete Sermons of John Wesley by John Wesley
Introduction to the Devout Life by Francis de Sales
Directions for Daily Communion by Matthew Henry
Heart Talks on Holiness by Samuel Logan Brendle
Holiness by J. C. Ryle
The Kneeling Christian by an anonymous author
The Pursuit of God by A. W. Tozer

All of these works were written by imperfect humans, so we need to read them the way we eat a fish—watching out for the bones. I've quoted from these works throughout this book. In doing so, I'm not implying that I agree with everything these men taught or practiced. Rather, I'm saying that they spoke well on the particular subject at hand.

Many of the people who best lived the Kingdom Life—such as the Waldensians, Czech Brethren, and early Anabaptists—didn't have the luxury of writing books about it. They were constantly fleeing from intense persecution, and so they had to devote their energies into trying to keep their movements together. When they did write, they were usually having to establish and defend what their movements believed.

The best way to read devotional classics is prayerfully. As we read, we should reflect on how each passage applies to us personally. We should let the authors challenge us to a closer walk with God and to a more complete surrender of our lives.

Worship

I personally don't schedule a time of worship (beyond praise and thanksgiving) in my devotional hour. However, often it just happens. I may be reading Scripture or a devotional classic or I may be in the middle of prayer, and I'm so overwhelmed with God's presence and His goodness that I want to just worship Him. William Law describes it this way, "Sometimes the light of God's countenance shines so bright upon us, we see so far into the invisible world, we are so affected with the wonders of the love and goodness of God, that our hearts worship and adore in a language higher than that of words, and we feel the ecstatic joy of worship."[27] May your devotional hour transport you to those heights as well!

Close With Prayer

After we have read both the Scriptures and a portion of a worthwhile spiritual classic, we will likely find that we have a lot more things to talk about with God: new resolutions to make based on what we've read; spiritual needs in our lives of which you've just become aware; sins we need to confess; thanksgiving for the insights we've been receiving. We should close our devotional time by praying to God about these things.

Satan's Designs

Because our devotional hour is such an important part of the Kingdom Life, Satan will do whatever he can to torpedo our devotional time. I can speak from experience, as it has happened to me.

15

The Lord's Pig

The devil will rob us of this hour if we do not steadfastly fight for it. –Samuel Logan Brengle

Once having begun the habit, never give it up. –J. C. Ryle

Many years ago, Deborah and I were looking into starting a micro-loan ministry in Jamaica. We knew of the great poverty that persisted throughout the island, and we wanted to enable the poor to break free from their endless cycle. We had written the Jamaican government and told them what we had in mind. So when we arrived in Jamaica, a government official met with us, and we spent the next several days visiting various villages in Jamaica's interior with the government official as our driver.

As we got to know the official, we discovered that he was a committed Christian. So we enjoyed good spiritual conversation during our time with him. Our most interesting conversation was about something that happened in his church. The story concerned a poor Jamaican, Joe Williams, and his wife Natalie (not their real names). Joe and Natalie were so poor that the only asset to their names was a sow. They planned on having the sow bred and then raising and selling her litter to earn some much-needed money.

However, before they were able to follow through with their plans, the sow became very ill. Sadly, Joe and Natalie had no money to hire a veterinarian. The sow's condition became steadily worse, so the next Sunday Joe and

Natalie asked their congregation to pray about the matter. Joe stood up and made a pledge before the congregation. He promised that if God answered their prayers favorably and their sow recovered, they would donate one of the sow's offspring to the Lord. This pig would be the Lord's pig. Joe and Natalie would raise it, and then when it was old enough, they would give it to the church. The church could sell it or to do whatever it wanted with it.

The congregation prayed fervently on behalf of the young couple, and the Lord answered their prayers. The sow recovered, and eventually Joe and Natalie had her bred. After about three-and-a-half months, Joe started going out early each morning to see if the litter had been born yet. He checked day after day, but no litter. Until one morning when he went out, he saw the sow lying on her side with a litter of piglets happily nursing. Joe was so happy he could hardly contain his excitement. He just stood there and watched in delight.

As his eyes scanned the pigpen, he noticed one small piglet lying by itself off to the side, not moving. Apparently it had been stillborn. Joe studied the scene for a few moments. He then shouted to his wife, "Natalie, Natalie, come quick! Something terrible has happened!"

Natalie came running out of the house, drying her hands on her apron. "What's happened? Did the sow die?"

"No, it's much worse than that!" Joe exclaimed.

"Worse than that? What is it then?" Natalie inquired.

With enormous emotion in his voice and tears welling in his eyes, Joe cried out, "The Lord's pig died!"

Am I Joe Williams?

When our friend finished the story, Deborah and I shook our heads in disbelief. *What a hypocrite!* we both thought.

For years afterward, I thought about Joe Williams and the story of the Lord's pig. In fact, I frequently told the story to others. However, I couldn't imagine this narrative ever having any application in *my* life. Surely *I* would never make a commitment to God and then renege on it.

However, about ten years after I first heard this story, something happened that made me see the incident in an entirely different light. Over the years, our family had established a tradition of having a devotional time each evening before bedtime. We tried to read all the way through the One Year Bible annually. So part of our devotional time each evening was set aside for that day's allotted Bible reading. After reading, we would all take turns praying. The entire devotional period usually lasted twenty to thirty minutes.

One evening, our youngest son and I were working on a puzzle together. It was a large puzzle, and it was taking us much longer than I had anticipated. But since we were so close to finishing, I didn't want to stop. At long last we completed it. But when I looked at the clock, I realized it was way past bedtime.

"Oh, that's too bad," I told the family. "We're not going to be able to have our Bible reading tonight. Nor is there time for each of us to pray. It's much too late. I'll just say a prayer for all of us, and then let's all head to bed."

I didn't think much about canceling our devotional time, as this sort of thing had happened before. However, as I lay in bed that night, the Holy Spirit convicted me.

I suddenly realized that I was no different than Joe Williams. Our devotional time every evening was supposed to be the Lord's time. I had been presented with a choice that evening. When I saw that we weren't going to be able to finish the puzzle in time, I could have let *my* pig die. I could have said, "Oh, too bad, but we're not going to be able to finish the puzzle tonight." But, no, I was just like Joe Williams: "Oh, how terrible! The Lord's pig died. We simply are unable to have our devotional time tonight."

The more I thought about it, the more I realized that I had been guilty of that kind of thing repeatedly. Unexpected things came up many evenings. The result? Somehow it was always the Lord's pig that died. "Oops! No time for Bible reading tonight." It was never one of my pigs.

So for the family devotional time to work, I saw I needed to make a firm commitment that when unexpected things happened, it would be *our* pig that would die. It wouldn't be the Lord's pig. Otherwise, we would find that time after time, we would end up neglecting our devotional time. Like Joe Williams, we would end up saying, "Oh, no! The Lord's pig died!"

The Personal Devotional Hour

In this chapter I've been talking about our *family* devotional time. But the same principle is true with regard to someone's personal devotional time. Rest assured, Satan will do what he can to throw a monkey wrench into your devotional hour so that it won't become a fixed habit. People will call you or come by to see you. Issues will arise at work or in the family. If you don't make a firm resolve to keep your devotional hour and contend for it, it will soon become little more than an ideal of what you would like to do but rarely have time to.

Twentieth century spiritual writer Anthony Bloom shares this insight on faithfully maintaining your devotional hour:

> Ask yourself this question: does the salvation of the world truly depend on the letter you are writing, the copper you are cleaning, or the words full of wisdom that you are in the midst of pronouncing? Did the world not exist for many years before you said or did this or that? Will it not still live many years without your continuing to be a useful presence?
>
> So give it a chance now to enjoy your absence. Settle peacefully and say: "Whatever happens, I will not budge." Say to all who come to disturb you, whether visible persons or invisible thoughts: "I am very sorry. I am here, but not for you."[28]

Despite the fact that the devotional hour is of such vital importance, there is another secret of the Kingdom Life that will perhaps have an even greater effect on your spiritual walk: continual communion with God.

16

Continual Communion with God

We cultivate our fields, praising. We sail the sea, singing hymns. – Clement of Alexandria

Paul bids us to "pray without ceasing" (1 Thess. 5:17). Obviously, Paul doesn't mean never sleeping or conversing with other people. But he does mean we should be continually praying as much as possible throughout the day. In this manner, we stay in constant communion with God.

When we finish our morning prayers, we should pursue our daily activities like a small child going on a walk with his father on the beach. With one hand, the child picks up seashells and other interesting objects. With the other hand, he holds tightly to his father's hand. Whether we're at home or out in the world, we should go through each day consciously holding God's hand as we proceed. But how do we do this?

We do this by pouring out numerous short prayers to God throughout the day. "Father, help me avert my eyes from anything that might stir up lust or covetousness." "Father, thank you for giving me the strength not to look at the racy magazine covers as I walked by that newsstand." "Father, help me to purge from my mind the gossip I just heard." "Father, I realize I was very impatient with my co-worker just now. Please forgive me." "Father,

I just learned that Susan's husband is in the hospital. Please heal him and speed his recovery. And please give Susan and the children extra strength at this time." "Father, I praise you for this lovely earth you created."

These prayers do not have to be long. Just one or two sentences keeps you in constant fellowship with the Father. Even if you find long times of prayer difficult during your devotional hour, you may discover that you excel at these short, constant prayers throughout the day.

Don't worry about using special phrases or exalted language. Just address whatever needs you have at the moment. Give thanks for every blessing you receive. Share your every concern with God. Intercede for every person you come into contact with during that day. Even though you will be making a nightly examination with God, confess your sins as soon as you become aware of them, and then ask forgiveness. Of course, you can't expect God's forgiveness if you're not truly repentant. He sees through fake repentance in an instant. And if you're not continuously forgiving others for their sins throughout the day, you can't expect forgiveness for your sins (Matt. 6:15).

This is what it means to "pray without ceasing." It doesn't require us to be on our knees the whole day. Rather, it means we keep our morning prayer going throughout the whole day through these short bursts of petitions, praises, confessions, and intercessions. Matthew Henry compares our early morning prayer to lighting a fire on the family altar. We need to keep that fire going throughout the day, never letting it get cold. So we must keep adding sticks to the fire by sending up short prayers and praises throughout the day. Thereby, we make our whole day one continuous prayer.

The early Christians prayed as they dressed. They prayed as they walked to their jobs. They prayed as they worked. Most of them had common jobs doing manual labor. And this was ideal. It meant that their minds were free all day to pray to God. They sang hymns as they plowed their fields or mended their fishing nets. They prayed as they washed their families' clothes and cooked their meals. Clement of Alexandria said this about the man who lives the Kingdom Life: "His whole life is prayer and conversation with God."[29]

Maintaining an Awareness of God's Presence

Communing with God throughout the day means more than just sending up prayers continually. We should also maintain an awareness of God's presence at all times. It doesn't matter whether we're talking with Him or not. He is right there with us. He's standing beside us when we wash the dishes. He's sitting next to us as we drive. He's standing next to us at work.

He's not there as Big Brother, hoping to catch us in some sin. He's there as a Father, looking lovingly on all that we do. He's also watching over us with loving concern when we fail. To be sure, He doesn't wink at sin. Yet He's not a harsh judge waiting to throw the book at us with every wrong step. He wants to work with us, not against us.

Nearly all Christians know God is always present with us. That is, they know it *intellectually*. But knowing His continuous presence *experientially*, that's a different matter. For most of us it takes years and years of discipline, concentration, and spiritual growth before we reach a place where we are as aware of His presence as we are of another person standing in the room.

We've talked a lot about prayer in the last few chapters because it is such an extremely crucial part of the Kingdom Life. And so is obedience. So in the next section, let's talk about obedience.

THE ROLE OBEDIENCE PLAYS

17

The Proof Is in the Fruit

How am I to know the authentic from the imitation? It is a general rule concerning feelings and affections that their test is in their fruits. –Francis of Sales

Imitation Christianity is one of the greatest obstacles to living the genuine Kingdom Life. How do we know the imitation from the real thing? Jesus gave us a simple but perfect test: "By their fruits you will know them" (Matt. 7:20). Once we get past the excitement and pious expressions someone makes, what do we find? Do we see the fruits of the Spirit? Do we find "love, joy, peace, longsuffering, kindness, goodness, faithfulness, gentleness, and self-control"? (Gal. 5:22-23). Authentic Christianity produces these fruits.

Producing godly fruit and obeying Christ are inextricably linked. John tells us, "Now by this we know that we know Him, if we keep His commandments. He who says, 'I know Him,' and does not keep His commandments, is a liar, and the truth is not in him" (1 John 2:3-4). Strong words indeed!

It's easy to proclaim to everyone how much we love Jesus. It's easy to be infatuated with the image of Jesus and to have warm, rapturous thoughts whenever we think of Him. But is it true love? The test of whether or not we truly love Jesus comes down to one thing: *Do we keep His commandments?* If we don't, we are only imagining we love Him. John tells us further, "In this the children of God and the children of the devil are manifest: Whoever does not practice righteousness is not of God" (1 John 3:10).

Because imitation spirituality is not something new, men of God through the ages have written a lot about it. Sixteenth-century Anabaptist leader Dirk Philips writes, "Not everyone who claims the new birth and prattles on about the new creature is in fact a person reborn from God. It is only the person who has taken on the godly character and nature of Jesus Christ."[30]

Scottish minister Henry Scougal described counterfeit spirituality in his day: "Some put all religion in the affections, in rapturous hearts, and ecstatic devotion. All they aim at is to pray with passion, to think of heaven with pleasure, and to be touched by those kind and melting expressions by which they court their Savior. Eventually, they persuade themselves they are mightily in love with Him."[31]

Nineteenth-century preacher J. C. Ryle observed, "You may weep under preaching one day, and be lifted to the third heaven by joyous excitement another day, and yet be dead to God."[32] Twentieth-century Christian writer George Otis, Jr. has observed, "Many, many have wept at church altars only to arise unchanged and eventually engage themselves in the same sins over which they wept."[33] Hymn writer Isaac Watts complained of those in his day who "seem to make all their faith consist of a few warm and pious feelings."[34]

So although it is right to love God with our emotions, if our "love" consists of emotions alone, it is not real love. Jesus tells us quite plainly, "He who has My commandments and keeps them, it is he who loves Me" (John 14:21). But if we're going to live the Kingdom Life, one of the important things we must understand is that not all obedience is the same.

Different Types of Obedience

Christians obey God's commandments for various reasons. Many Christians obey His laws mainly out of fear of punishment or desire for reward. Others obey because they appreciate what Christ has done for them and they want to be His obedient, dutiful servants. However, another secret of the Kingdom Life is that we must not only obey God's law, but we should actually *love* His laws. Surrendered Christians are glad that God has given us His laws, for they are convinced that His laws produce the happiest and best way to live.

Although human governments don't care what motivates our obedience, God cares very much about our motivation. In His kindness He accepts all three of these types of obedience: 1) fear obedience, 2) dutiful servant obedience, and 3) love obedience. However, fear obedience and dutiful servant obedience are both less than God's best for us. God wants to help us grow to the point where we obey Him because we love His laws. Only then do we truly discover that His commandments are not burdensome.

In the next few chapters we're going to look at these three types of obedience in detail and see what factors distinguish love obedience from the other two.

18

Type 1: Fear Obedience

Those slavish spirits will be sure to do no more than is absolutely required. For it is a law that compels them. –Henry Scougal

They formally renounce and forsake sinful acts, but they turn back many a fond lingering look to what they have left, like Lot's wife as she fled from Sodom. –Francis of Sales

We'll begin with Type 1 obedience—obedience motivated by fear. Type 1 Christians correctly understand that without holiness "no one will see the Lord" (Heb. 12:14). They realize that obedience to God is not optional, that we must bear fruit to stay on the Vine. They also recognize that obedience to Christ's commandments is part of bearing fruit. All of these things are commendable.

However, Type 1 Christians obey Christ's teachings primarily out of fear of eternal punishment. One writer described his life as a Type 1 Christian in these words: "For years I lived for myself. All my hopes and ambitions centered in myself; even my desire to go to heaven was more a desire to escape from the pains of hell than to enjoy the society of Jesus and redeemed souls, and to do good and be holy."[35]

To be sure, fear is often the starting point of living an obedient life. Obedience stemming from fear is better than disobedience. In fact, Christ repeatedly gives us warnings and uses fear to motivate us to obey. He alerts us to eternal danger, saying: "If your right eye causes you to sin, pluck it out and cast it from you; for it is more profitable for you that one of your members perish, than for your whole body to be cast into hell. And if your right hand causes you to sin, cut it off and cast it from you; for it is more profitable for you that one of your members perish, than for your whole body to be cast into hell" (Matt. 5:29-30).

So Christ accepts obedience that is primarily motivated by fear. In fact, the Scriptures tell us, "The fear of the Lord is the beginning of wisdom." But that's the point—it's only the *beginning* of wisdom. Christ wants us to grow to the point where we obey His commandments because we love Him, not because we fear Him.

Druscilla Dread

Druscilla Dread is a Type 1 Christian. After hearing an impassioned sermon about the horrors of hell, she gave her life to Christ when she was a teenager. Since then she has read the many warnings in Scripture against disobedience, and she has taken them to heart. So she lives a very careful, restricted life based on fear. She would never dream of committing immorality, getting drunk, taking illegal drugs, stealing, using profanity, or a whole host of other sins.

Yet Druscilla constantly wears a dour face, for her Christian walk is joyless. In her heart she loves much of the world and is attracted to its pleasures. She wishes she could participate in its enjoyments. However, fear of God holds her back. An intense war rages inside Druscilla because she is divided between Christ and the world. Although she would never admit it, Druscilla envies the lives of many of her unsaved neighbors. In fact, she would live like them but for fear of the judgment to come. William Law astutely describes Type 1 Christians like Druscilla:

> While you are divided between God and the world, you have neither the pleasures of Christianity, nor the pleasures of the world, but are always in the uneasiness of a divided state of heart. . . . You have only so much Christianity as serves to disquiet you, but not Christianity enough to give you a taste and feeling of its pleasures. . . . So that you are just as happy as the slave that dares not run away from his master, and yet always serves him against his will.[36]

That's exactly what Druscilla is—a slave who serves her Master out of fear. She wishes she could run away from her Master, but she's afraid to. So there is little joy in her Christian walk. She hasn't found Christ's yoke to be easy or His burden light. In fact, her life would be almost unbearable if it weren't for the fact that she's found a way to "game the system." Or at least she thinks she has.

Christ's denunciation of the scribes and Pharisees in Matthew 23 hasn't been lost on Druscilla. She often thinks about Jesus' words to the Pharisees: "You pay tithe of mint and anise and cummin but have neglected the weightier matters of the law" (Matt. 23:23). Druscilla correctly realizes that not all Biblical commandments are on the same level. Some are weightier than others, as Jesus said. In fact, Jesus even talked about the two *greatest* commandments. So some commandments are obviously more important than others.

To be sure, all sin is equal in the sense that, apart from our redemption through Christ's shed blood, any sin bars us from eternal life. Even the smallest sin means that we are deserving of death. And we are utterly unable to save ourselves, even if the only sins we have committed are relatively minor ones. However, after we have been saved—after we have become branches on the Vine—then all sins are not the same. When Jesus examines our fruit, He is particularly looking at the weightier matters. This is clear from his interaction with the scribes and Pharisees.

Paul also makes it clear that not all sins are on the same level. He warns us that those who practice certain sins will not inherit the kingdom of God. "Do you not know that the unrighteous will not inherit the kingdom of God? Do not be deceived. Neither fornicators, nor idolaters, nor adulterers, nor homosexuals, nor sodomites, nor thieves, nor covetous, nor drunkards, nor revilers, nor extortioners will inherit the kingdom of God" (1 Cor. 6:9-10; see also Gal. 5:19-21).

Druscilla has reviewed this list many times, as it is a great comfort to her. "I'm certainly no fornicator, adulterer, homosexual, sodomite, or extortioner!" Druscilla consoles herself. "And I've never worshiped an idol, been drunk, or stolen anything." Druscilla doesn't even know what a reviler is, but she's quite certain she's not one. She acknowledges to herself that *occasionally* she's coveted something not belonging to her. "But that hardly makes me covetous," she says in self-defense. "Everyone occasionally covets something they can't have or afford."

Yes, Druscilla takes great comfort in the fact that her sins aren't on the list of offenses that will keep us from inheriting the kingdom. "Those things that Paul mentions are *salvation issues*," she often explains to others. "If we're guilty of those practices and are unrepentant, then we will eventually be cut off the Vine." And Druscilla is technically correct. However, how she applies this principle is not what Paul had in mind.

For example, last month Druscilla took another believer to court over some money he owed her. Elizabeth, a concerned Christian who knows Druscilla, spoke to Druscilla about this inconsistency. "I thought you believed in obeying what the Scriptures teach," she said. "Don't you know the Scriptures say that Christians shouldn't take one another to court?" Elizabeth then read to Druscilla the following passage in 1 Corinthians:

> Dare any of you, having a matter against another, go to law before the unrighteous, and not before the saints? Do you not know that the saints will judge the world? And if the world will be judged by you, are you unworthy to judge the smallest matters? Do you not know that we shall judge angels? How much more, things that pertain to this life? (1 Cor. 6:1-3).

"Well, technically you're right," Druscilla conceded. "No, I shouldn't have taken him to court. However, taking a brother to court is not a *salvation issue*. So I'm not going to worry about it. He owed me over $5,000. Nobody cheats Druscilla Dread and gets away with it! Besides, when someone behaves like he did, I seriously question whether he can truly be called a brother."

Rightly Dividing the Word?

Druscilla has given new meaning to "dividing the word of truth" (2 Tim. 2:15). She has mentally divided all the commandments of Scripture into two groups: those that she believes are "salvation issues" and those that aren't. She is extremely careful not to break those commandments that she views as salvation issues.

As for the other commandments, she picks and chooses obedience based on the level of inconvenience and sacrifice involved. If the cost to her isn't too great, she obeys them. But if the cost is substantial, she ignores them. She took another Christian to court because she felt that $5,000 was just too big of a sacrifice. And she will carefully point out to you that Paul never said that those who take their brother to court will not inherit the kingdom of God.

So what do you think of Druscilla Dread? Has she found a shortcut to make Jesus' yoke easy without living the Kingdom Life? Has she outsmarted Christ? Before you answer those questions, let me introduce you to Sammy Slick.

19

Sammy Slick

For a moment imagine that you've just started work at Grimm's Hardware Store. The owner, Malcolm Grimm, introduces you to Sammy Slick, with whom you'll be working closely. "Sammy will teach you the ropes," Mr. Grimm explains. "He's a pleasant fellow, and you'll enjoy working with him."

And sure enough, you find Sammy a very congenial fellow. You have many good conversations with him, and the two of you laugh a lot. However, you soon notice that Sammy doesn't follow all the workplace rules.

"Sammy, I hate to say anything," you mention discretely late one afternoon, "but I notice that you nearly always quit work around 4:50 or 4:55. Mr. Grimm told me that we don't get off until 5:00. Aren't you afraid you're going to get into trouble?"

"Oh, I'm sure old man Grimm doesn't like me leaving early, but I can guarantee you he's not going to *fire* me over it," Sammy asserts confidently. He then puts away his tools and heads for his car—five minutes early.

You've also noticed that Sammy takes about seventy to seventy-five minutes each day for lunch. You remember quite distinctly Mr. Grimm telling you that employees are allowed one hour for lunch. "Say, Sammy," you finally mention, "I'm sure Mr. Grimm told me that we get an hour lunch break. But you always take nearly an hour and a quarter. Aren't you afraid you'll get caught one of these days and get into trouble?"

"Oh, I'm sure old man Grimm knows what I'm doing," Sammy replies dismissively. "But he's not going to *fire* me over it. So I don't worry about it."

As the weeks pass, you notice that Sammy frequently takes personal calls and texts on his cell phone during work. Often when you need his help with something, you have to wait until he gets off the phone. "Listen, Sammy," you finally say, "don't you think you're going to get in trouble one of these days for spending so much time on your cell phone?"

Shaking his head impatiently, Sammy replies, "What are you—a Boy Scout or something? Yeah, I imagine they don't like me talking and texting on my cell phone. But believe me, they're not going to *fire* me over it. So quit worrying."

Over time, you notice more and more company rules that Sammy violates. By now, you've quit bringing such matters up to him, for you know what his reply will be: "Yeah, I'm not supposed to do it, but they're not going to *fire* me over it."

Sammy Slick Syndrome

So what do you think about Sammy Slick? If you were an employer, would you like to have someone like him working for you? Would you think that Sammy cherishes the relationship he has with you as his employer? Obviously not.

To be sure, Sammy obeys every rule he thinks he'd be fired for breaking. But he stretches or breaks most of the rules he thinks he can get away with. As Sammy has shrewdly calculated, the owner is probably not going to fire him over any single one of these infractions. However, the owner may eventually tire of the attitude that

Sammy's actions reveal. Sammy obviously doesn't have the company's best interests at heart.

Type 1 Christians typically play the "salvation issue" game. They obey all the big commandments—they don't commit adultery, fornication, murder, blasphemy, robbery, etc. However, they feel comfortable ignoring the smaller commandments. As we've said before, their primary motivation is fear of eternal punishment—not love of God and His commandments.

A primary problem with Type 1 Christians is their heart condition. Jesus talked a lot about the heart when He was on earth. In the parable of the sower, this is how He described the ones who would faithfully bear fruit on the Vine: "The ones that fell on the good ground are those who, having heard the word *with a noble and good heart*, keep it and bear fruit with patience" (Luke 8:15).

Why Druscilla Dread's Strategy Doesn't Work

Druscilla Dread is right to put more emphasis on the weightier commandments than on the minor ones. However, she has ignored two important precepts in Jesus' denunciation of the Pharisees in Matthew 23. First, notice what Jesus designated to be the weightier commandments: "You have neglected the weightier matters of the law: justice and mercy and faith" (Matt. 23:23). To be sure, adultery and murder are weighty matters, but what Jesus specifically referred to were qualities inside the heart—justice, mercy, and faith. These qualities are not simple matters of do this and don't do that. They come out of a godly heart.

Jesus developed this point more fully in another passage: "A good tree does not bear bad fruit, nor does a bad tree bear good fruit. For every tree is known by its own fruit. For men do not gather figs from thorns, nor do they gather grapes from a bramble bush. A good man out of the good treasure of his heart brings forth good; and an evil man out of the evil treasure of his heart brings forth evil. For out of the abundance of the heart his mouth speaks. But why do you call Me 'Lord, Lord,' and do not do the things which I say?" (Luke 6:43-46).

So trying to be a Druscilla Dread on the eternal playing field doesn't work. Bearing good fruit has to come out of a cleansed heart closely in tune with God. Merely avoiding committing the "big sins" isn't sufficient. That alone will not produce good fruit.

Furthermore, we should remember what Jesus identified as the two greatest commandments: "You shall love the Lord your God with all your heart, with all your soul, with all your mind, and with all your strength. This is the first commandment. And the second, like it, is this: 'You shall love your neighbor as yourself.' There is no other commandment greater than these" (Mark 12:30-31). Can Druscilla possibly claim that she loves God with all of her heart, soul, mind, and strength? How can she when her primary motivation is self-preservation, not love for God? Sammy Slick might just as well claim that he loves Grimm's Hardware Store with his whole heart, soul, mind, and strength.

So although Type 1 obedience is where we might begin our Christian walk, it's not a place we want to dwell. We will never be able to live the Kingdom Life with Type 1 obedience. So let's move on to Type 2, dutiful servant obedience.

20

Type 2: Dutiful Servant Obedience

These are those who "are of God." Yet they are not properly sons, but servants. They depart from evil, study to do good, and walk in all His ordinances, because they have the fear of God in their heart and a sincere desire to please Him. –John Wesley

They may not commit great sins. They may be trying to do right. But so long as they serve God from duty, and do not know Him as their Father and the Joy of their being, they are slaves—good slaves, but slaves. –George MacDonald

Type 2 obedience is that of a dutiful servant. Type 2 Christians live moral, upright lives because they want to be obedient to their Master. They don't want to do anything that displeases Him. However, their obedience is primarily motivated by *submission* to God, not *love* of God. Their obedience often flows more from their minds, or from their sense of duty, than it does from their hearts.

Timothy Toiler

Timothy Toiler is a classic Type 2 Christian. He has a fairly consistent spiritual walk, and most others in his church view him as a very committed Christian. And in many senses, Timothy is. He doesn't pick and choose which commandments of Christ to keep, for he knows that none of them are optional. Furthermore, fear of hell is not what motivates him, but a genuine desire to obey Christ as his Lord.

So what more could Jesus want? To be sure, Christ accepts Timothy's obedience and is pleased with Him. However, Timothy is still largely a stranger to the Kingdom Life. He shoulders most of the responsibilities of being a Christian, but he misses out on most of Christianity's joys. Timothy certainly doesn't find Christ's yoke to be easy nor His burden to be light. What's missing?

What's missing is any love for God's commandments. Timothy's primary motivation is the desire that a faithful, obedient servant has to please his master. However, Christ calls us to a much deeper and more satisfying relationship than merely being His servant. Not only does Timothy not love Christ's commands, he doesn't particularly *like* most of them. In fact, he would be glad if Christ abolished them. However, since Christ has not canceled them, Timothy will dutifully obey Christ's commands.

What If The Bible Wasn't True?

One day Timothy Toiler was talking with Bill, one of his Christian friends, about different "what if" situations. In the course of the conversation, Bill asked Timothy, "What if it turned out the Bible wasn't true? Do you think you'd still live the godly life you live now?"

Timothy thought for a moment and then replied, "For the most part, yes. However, I have to admit that there are a lot of things I do only because the Bible commands them."

"Such as?" Bill asked.

"Well, I certainly wouldn't turn the other cheek if Jesus hadn't commanded it. I've been cheated in business dealings a number of times. How I would relish taking those people to court!"

"Anything else?"

Timothy reflected for a moment. "When I'm in the break room at work, I hate the fact that I'm usually out of touch with the conversations around me. The other employees talk about the latest movie or rock star or something like that. I usually have no idea what they're talking about. Or they're telling some risqué story or off-color joke, and I have to move to an empty corner to get away from it. I feel like I'm missing out on so much fun. Others are doing so many exciting things that I can't do because I'm a Christian."

"I know exactly what you mean," Bill concurred, nodding.

Yes, Timothy would rather live by the world's standards . . . if only God permitted it. However, he's a dutiful servant, and so he lives by God's commandments. He doesn't go to the latest movies, but he wishes he could. He doesn't join in the office football pool, but he wishes he could. He doesn't cheat on his taxes, but he wishes he could.

Timothy believes that he loves God with all of his heart, soul, mind, and strength because he obeys God's commandments. "I don't particularly love God's *commandments*," he will admit. "But I do love *God*." And perhaps Timothy does love God with all of his mind, but He doesn't love God with all of his heart and soul. Let me explain.

What's Missing in Timothy's Life?

Timothy Toiler is a born-again Christian, and I believe that Christ accepts Timothy's type of obedience. In fact, no doubt Timothy receives many blessings from Christ in his life. Like Type 1 fear obedience, Type 2 dutiful servant obedience may be where many Christians *start*. Or perhaps it represents the next step in their spiritual growth.

It certainly is better than fear obedience. However, it's not where Christ wants us to *dwell.*

I think if we're honest, almost all of us will have to admit that some of our obedience is dutiful servant compliance. Very few, if any, of us ever reach true love obedience in every facet of our lives. Even Paul acknowledged, "I buffet my body and make it my slave, lest possibly, after I have preached to others, I myself should be disqualified" (1 Cor. 9:27 NAS). So if Paul had to discipline himself and make his body his slave, none of us should imagine that we're going to reach a state of complete surrender to Christ without having to discipline ourselves as well. However, we should not have to 'buffet our bodies' in order to obey most of Christ's commands.

Christians like Timothy Toiler make the sacrifice of denying themselves for Christ, but they receive only part of the joy and refreshment that comes from love obedience, where Christ's yoke is easy and His burden is light. Sometimes Type 2 obedience produces a cold and spiritless Christianity. Timothy Toiler makes me think of someone in the olden days in an arranged marriage where neither spouse really loved the other. They dutifully carried out the responsibilities of married life, and they were faithful to each other. Yet they didn't enjoy a vibrant, joyful marriage where warmth and love abounded.

The Danger of Burn Out

What most Christians find is that it's difficult to remain at Type 2 obedience throughout their entire lives. They need to move on to the Kingdom Life with its love obedience. Here they will experience the joys that Christ has promised, and His easy yoke will become a reality for them. However, most Type 2 Christians don't turn to the Kingdom Life. Instead, often they burn out at some point. The pews of thousands of churches and the sofas of thousands of homes are littered with the spiritual corpses of burned-out Type 2 Christians.

What happens when Type 2 Christians burn out? Some give up on Christianity altogether. Others turn into Type 1 Christians, obeying only those commandments that they perceive as being "salvation issues." Others turn into pharisaic Christians. They follow the letter of the law and then attempt to lighten their burden by looking down on all other Christians they perceive as being less spiritual. They receive carnal, unholy pleasure by feeling superior to others. They may even imagine that they are now living the Kingdom Life. However, those truly living the Kingdom Life aren't fault finders, and they don't look down on others.

Still other burned-out Type 2 Christians "discover grace." They tell themselves that they've been in legal bondage for years, and so they decide that the popular Christianity of easy-believism is right after all. Now they only obey those commands they find easy. They imagine at long last they have found "freedom in Christ." The yoke upon them is now easy and the burden is light—but only because they ignore any commandments that are burdensome to them.

Yes, dutiful servant obedience is a difficult place to dwell. That's why it's important to move forward into love obedience.

21

Type 3: Love Obedience

He keeps all the commandments of God, and he does so with all his might. For his obedience is in proportion to his love, the source from which it flows. –John Wesley

All His commands are for our benefit and founded in the necessities of our natures. They are only so many instructions to become more happy than we could be without them. –William Law

He will feel what Paul felt when he said, "I delight in the law of God after the inward man." – J. C. Ryle

In a small town in central Honduras, the local residents had always enjoyed eating ice cream on hot days. At least, they *thought* they enjoyed eating ice cream. However, it turns out that what they believed to be ice cream was actually only "frozen dessert," containing little or no cream or milk fat. It was imitation ice cream. However, no one realized it because they had never had the real thing.

Then some missionaries from the United States opened an ice cream shop selling authentic ice cream. They made the ice cream from scratch using milk and cream from their own dairy herd. The profits supported a children's home they operated. Most of the local Hondurans had never tasted real ice cream before, and they immediately noticed the difference. As word got around, people thronged to the new ice cream shop. Once they tasted authentic ice cream, they didn't want to go back to imitation ice cream.

It's the same with love obedience. When all we've ever experienced is fear obedience or dutiful servant obedience, we may think we know what obedience to God is all about. However, the truth is that we've never tasted the real thing—love obedience. Fear obedience and dutiful servant obedience bring us most of the responsibilities of the Kingdom Life, but with only part of its blessings. Love obedience is both the easiest and most joyful way to walk with the Lord. It's one of the key secrets to the Kingdom Life.

But exactly what is love obedience?

Love Obedience

Love obedience flows from a deep, warm love relationship with Christ. It's the obedience of the Kingdom Life. When Christ abides in us thoroughly and completely, we obey Him out of love, not fear. Love obedience is the obedience of a *child*, rather than a mere *servant*.

To live the Kingdom Life, we not only need to obey God's commandments, but we need to actually *love* them. But why would we love them? It's because we believe that following God's laws is the best and happiest way to live. The Psalmist wrote, "Blessed is the man who fears the Lord, who delights greatly in His commandments" (Ps. 112:1). A lot of Christians fear the Lord. But how many can honestly say that they *delight* in His laws?

Of course this is the answer to the Great Paradox we spoke about at the beginning of the book. If we delight in Christ's laws, those laws prove to be a light burden. How can they be a heavy burden when we find pleasure in obeying them? This is another secret to the Kingdom Life—having *more* of Christ, not *less* of Him. The more we lose ourselves in Christ, the easier His yoke becomes.

Luke and Lydia Lovejoy

Luke and Lydia Lovejoy are living the Kingdom Life. Their obedience is marked by humility, kindness, love, and joy. They *want* to obey Christ because they know that God's laws are given for their good. They know that none of His laws are arbitrary commandments. Like other Christians living the Kingdom Life, they *love* God's laws.

As a result, the Lovejoys have made a commitment to follow *all* of God's laws. There's no picking and choosing for them. While they recognize that some commands are weightier than others, their desire is to follow *all* of Christ's commandments. They don't try to determine if a particular commandment is a "salvation issue," for they realize that our Lord never gave an unnecessary or an optional command. The Lovejoys know that every commandment of Christ was given solely out of His love for us. We can't reject His commandments without rejecting His love.

Discovering the Reasons Behind God's Commandments

Christians living the Kingdom Life want to understand *why* a commandment was given. To be sure, they will obey every one of Christ's commandments whether or not they understand the reason behind the command. But they will search for the reason, because they grasp that all of God's laws have a purpose. They know that His laws are part of the universe of Reality—the universe that God and His angels inhabit. God's laws stand in contrast to the universe of Unreality—the universe made up of this world, our fallen flesh, and Satan and his minions.

Medieval writer Richard of St. Victor made the following observation: "The Sermon on the Mount is neither impractical idealism nor a collection of unlivable moral precepts. It is a superb analysis of right action in the light of things as they really are and not as they appear to be."[37] The same can be said about all of Christ's commandments.

George MacDonald writes about Christians living the Kingdom Life, "Although the Lord would be pleased with any man for doing a thing because He said it, God will show He is pleased with this man by making him more and more dissatisfied until he knows *why* the Lord had said it. God wants him to see that he cannot obey any command in the deepest sense of the word until he sees the reasonableness of it.[38]

The Parable of the Three Bricklayers

In 1194, during the High Middle Ages, a visitor was ambling down the main street of Chartres, France. He walked through the marketplace, which was bustling with all kinds of commercial activities. In one area, the meat and vegetable sellers congregated, hawking their goods. In another area stood the textile merchants, displaying their colorful fabrics. Money changers sat on their benches, where they exchanged foreign currency for the local money. Wine merchants plied their wares.

As he walked past the market, this visitor spied a group of men laying bricks. Curious what they were working on, he approached the nearest bricklayer and said, "Excuse me, my fine fellow, but I'm curious what you're doing."

Without looking up, the worker curtly replied, "I'm laying bricks."

That didn't really answer the visitor's question, so he walked over to the second bricklayer and asked him the same thing. "Excuse me, but could you tell me what you're doing?"

Without missing a beat, the second worker replied, "Can't you see that I'm laying bricks?"

Growing frustrated, the visitor finally walked up to the third laborer and said, "I hate to bother you, sir, but I'm curious as to what you're doing." The third worker turned around, smiling, and with a gleam in his eye proudly announced, "I'm building a cathedral."

Seeing the Big Picture

When it comes to God's commandments, Christians who live the Kingdom Life look at the big picture. The first two workers in our story could only think of the immediate task at hand—laying bricks. That's all their job meant to them. However, the third worker saw the bigger picture, building a cathedral. As a result, he received a sense of joy and accomplishment from his work that the other two men didn't. It's the same with those who live the Kingdom Life. They look at the bigger picture and the *purpose* of God's various commandments. This gives them an appreciation and joy for His commands. As a result they find that God's commands are not grievous or burdensome.

Love Obedience Versus Servant Obedience

When I was in my twenties, Deborah and I had a friend who played violin in the local community orchestra. The entire orchestra was made up of unpaid volunteers who played because of their love for music. Even the conductor worked without pay. The orchestra gave free concerts every year in order to introduce live classical music to our community. One day our musician friend told us about an event that well illustrates the difference between love obedience and servant obedience.

The orchestra was going to perform a concert that required certain musical instruments that were underrepresented within the community orchestra. So they hired musicians from the symphony orchestra of a nearby city to fill in the gaps. One night when they were rehearsing, the local conductor was not quite satisfied with how the orchestra was playing a certain work. The concert was only a few days away, and he wanted to smooth out some of the rough edges. So he had the musicians play the piece over and over, trying to get everything perfect. As a result, the rehearsal went longer than planned.

The orchestra was making considerable progress when suddenly the hired musicians stopped playing and began putting their instruments away into their cases. The conductor was bewildered, and so he asked the musicians what was happening. One of them explained they were all union members, and under their union contract they could not be required to rehearse past ten at night. With that, they walked off the stage and made their way to the parking lot.

The volunteer musicians were playing purely for their love of music. They were quite willing to stay late in order to get the musical piece just right. In contrast, the union musicians were hireling employees. They had arrived on time for the rehearsal and had played very well. But they weren't going to do one iota more than their contract required. Those playing out of love cared about the big picture—how the final concert was going to sound. The mercenary musicians were only looking at the terms of their contract. If the piece wasn't played quite perfectly at the coming concert, so be it.

Being Molded Into God's Image

Like the volunteer musicians, Christians living the Kingdom Life are interested in the big picture. They know that the ultimate purpose behind each New Testament commandment is to help mold us into the character of God. God wants to spend eternity only with people who are like Him. He wants to enjoy eternity with people who love the same things He loves and who detest the same things He detests. Imagine spending eternity with somebody who was utterly incompatible with you! If we have not been molded into God's image, then living with Him forever would be eternal punishment, not eternal bliss.

Because those living the Kingdom Life desire to be like God, they *want* God to mold them in His image. Therefore they welcome God's commandments. They know that God's commands help us to understand what He is truly like. And His commandments help us to know what we must do to become compatible with God.

An Example of the Big Picture

Let's analyze one of the New Testament commandments to see how things appear when we look at the big picture. We'll use the commandment God gives us in 1 John 2:15: "Do not love the world or the things in the world." That portion of the passage contains the entire commandment. What follows is not further commandments, but the explanation of *why* we must not love the world. John explains this to us: "If anyone loves the world, the love of the Father is not in him. For all that is in the world—the lust of the flesh, the lust of the eyes, and the pride of life—is not of the Father but is of the world. And the world is passing away, and the lust of it;

but he who does the will of God abides forever" (1 John 2:15-17).

So John points out that if we love the world, we don't have the love of the Father in us. As I said, this part of the passage is not a commandment. It's simply a statement of Reality. It gives us a good barometer by which we can measure our own hearts. If we find that we love the world and the things in it, then the love of God is not in us. It's that simple. Either we have never been born again, or else we aren't producing the fruit that God expects.

After an honest examination of ourselves, most of us will find that we love some things in the world but reject others. This tells us that (most likely) we *do* love God, but that our love is not perfect. We don't love God with our *whole* heart, soul, mind, and strength. I say that because once we reach that level of love, there will be no love of the world left in us. Why is that? Because everything the world values—the desires of the flesh and eyes, as well as the pride of life—are totally contrary to God.

Looking at Jesus

Because the Father dwells in the spirit realm, it's often hard for us humans to picture how He would respond to the everyday things we encounter. That was one of the reasons why the Son of God became man, so that we can see what Divinity looks like wearing sandals and walking on earth. As Jesus said, "He who has seen Me has seen the Father" (John 14:9).

Think about the character of the man Jesus for a moment. He was not tempted by sensuality, nor was He impressed by showmanship. He didn't look upon women with lust, nor did He try to attract attention to His own body. He had no desire to artificially make His body look different than His Father made it. In fact, this whole business of showing off one's material possessions to impress others was utterly foreign to Him. He coveted nothing, and He did nothing for the purpose of grabbing attention.

That's why John tells us, "If anyone loves the world, the love of the Father is not in him." John doesn't say this to burden us or to beat us down. He simply explains the way things are. When God's image is thoroughly stamped upon us, we'll view the world no differently than Jesus did when He was a man.

Now let's look at another example of how these three types of obedience play out in real life.

22

The Three Types of Obedience in Real Life

The vulgar, slavish, worldly idea of freedom thinks it consists in being bound to nothing. No such thing is God's idea of liberty!
–George MacDonald

Up to this point, we've talked about the three kinds of obedience in general terms. Now let's look at a specific New Testament commandment and see how our three representative people respond to this commandment. The commandment we're going to look at is from First Peter:

> Do not let your adorning be external—the braiding of hair and the putting on of gold jewelry, or the clothing you wear—but let your adorning be the hidden person of the heart with the imperishable beauty of a gentle and quiet spirit, which in God's sight is very precious. (1 Pet. 3:3-4, ESV)

Fear Obedience: Druscilla Dread

Druscilla Dread is always worried about the lake of fire the Bible talks about. She knows that no sacrifice in this life is too great to make in order to avoid eternal punishment. As Jesus said, it's better to cut off our right hand than to end up there. However, as we learned, Druscilla is also a pragmatist. She's certainly not going to make any sacrifices over things that she thinks will not cause her to lose her salvation.

"Dress plainly? Don't wear jewelry? Don't adorn myself?" she asks in disbelief. "Why, I wouldn't think of living that way."

One day another Christian pointed out to her what First Peter says. "Okay," Druscilla replied, "you may be right that I shouldn't adorn myself the way I do. But I'm not going to worry about it because it's not a *salvation issue.*" For Druscilla, that was the end of the matter.

Dutiful Obedience: Timothy and Tammy Toiler

As you'll recall, Timothy Toiler is a Type 2 Christian, who is a dutiful servant of Christ. His wife Tammy is the same. Together they are committed to living obediently to Christ their King, which is commendable. However, it's not love obedience. Tammy Toiler obeys the commands in 1 Peter that are directed to wives, just as Timothy obeys those directed to husbands. But Tammy doesn't *like* these commandments at all, and she can't see what purpose they serve. "I don't understand why I can't adorn myself with jewelry and upscale clothing," she complains. "What difference does it make to Christ?" Tammy sees no purpose or logic behind these commands.

Nevertheless, being an obedient servant of Christ, Tammy Toiler obeys these directives, although she goes no further than what the Scriptures actually say. To Timothy and Tammy, the New Testament commands are simply a list of do's and don'ts. They see no bigger picture than that. Christ no doubt accepts their obedience, but the Toilers miss out on much of the joy that comes with love obedience.

Love Obedience: Luke and Lydia Lovejoy

As Christians living the Kingdom Life, Luke and Lydia Lovejoy approach this commandment quite differently than the others. To begin with, there's never a question in their minds as to whether or not they will obey this command. Of course they will obey it. And they will do so with joy.

"What are the reasons behind this commandment?" they ask. "We know Christ didn't give us this command to be arbitrary, or to control us, or to make us different from other people. He gave us this commandment because He loves us. Its ultimate purpose is to help mold us into His image. So which attributes of Christ does this commandment address?"

Before seeking answers to their questions, the Lovejoys try to think of any parallel Scripture passages. The passage they immediately think of is 1 Timothy 2:8-10: "I desire therefore that the men pray everywhere, lifting up holy hands, without wrath and doubting; in like manner also, that the women adorn themselves in modest apparel, with propriety and moderation, not with braided hair or gold or pearls or costly clothing, but, which is proper for women professing godliness, with good works."

Luke and Lydia Lovejoy can't help noticing that Paul and Peter give almost identical directives. So what is the big picture behind these commands?

The Big Picture

After considerable reflection, the Lovejoys realize that the big picture is multi-faceted. The specific items mentioned (braided hair, gold, pearls, costly clothing) are like the bricks that make up a wall. That's all Timothy and Tammy Toiler see. They're like the two masons who couldn't visualize anything beyond laying bricks. However, Luke and Lydia Lovejoy realize that these "bricks" are intended to construct a beautiful cathedral, a soul that is completely remolded into the image of Christ. What are some aspects of such a soul?

Peter directs our attention to the first aspect—that we must focus on adorning our *soul*, not our physical body. He says, "Do not let your adorning be external . . . but let your adorning be the hidden person of the heart with the imperishable beauty of a gentle and quiet spirit, which in God's sight is very precious" (1 Pet. 3:3-4). This is no small matter, for it's at the center of the Kingdom Life. Is our focus on the inner man, which we adorn because it makes us beautiful in God's eyes? Or is our focus on our corruptible physical body, which we adorn because we want to impress other humans? Whose presence are we primarily conscious of? God's presence or the presence of other people? Do we adorn ourselves to please God or to please people?

If we adorn ourselves to please people, then we're going to adorn our outward physical body. The world places maximum value on external beauty. In the world, what's on the outside often counts far more than what's on the inside. When we humans look at a room full of people, we primarily see faces and bodies. In contrast, God primarily sees *hearts*. And we cannot adorn what God sees without changing our hearts (through Christ's power). Obviously, if our primary focus is on adorning our souls to appear beautiful before God, we're not going to disobey God and adorn ourselves on the outside. If we do that, we've just made our souls uglier.

Today when people think of plain dress and the rejection of outward adornment, they probably think of Mennonites, Amish, Brethren, and certain Pentecostal groups. However, in times past these commandments were closely obeyed by the Pilgrims, Puritans, Moravians, Quakers, Baptists, Presbyterians, and spiritually minded Methodists. One of the strongest sermons I've ever come across against adornment was preached by John Wesley. In his sermon, Wesley points out the discrepancy between outward adornment and inward holiness:

> Few can readily grasp the opposition there is between outward adorning and this inward quietness of spirit. You never can thoroughly enjoy this quietness of spirit while you are fond of outward adorning. It is only when you free yourself from outward adorning that you can in calmness possess your soul. Only when you have cast off your fondness for dress will the peace of God reign in your hearts.
>
> What's more, the putting on of costly apparel is directly opposite to what the apostle calls "the hidden man of the heart." It is opposite to the whole image of God in which we were created, and which is stamped anew upon the heart of every Christian believer. It is opposite to "the mind which was in Christ Jesus" and the whole nature of inward holiness.
>
> All the time you are studying this outward adorning, the whole inward work of the Spirit stands still. Not only that, it recedes. Instead of growing more heavenly-minded, you become more and more earthly-minded. If you once had fellowship with the Father and the Son, it now gradually declines and you sink deeper and deeper into the spirit of the world.[39]

Artificiality

The Lovejoys also realize that a soul that is molded into the image of Christ is also free of artificiality. Artificiality and Christ dwell in two separate realms. Everything that artificiality represents, Christ is not. This applies both to fake exterior spirituality and to fake exterior physical adornment. Twentieth-century preacher A. W. Tozer observed, "Advertising is largely based upon this habit of pretense. . . . Books are sold and clothes and cosmetics are peddled by playing continually upon this desire to appear what we are not."[40]

When we pretend to be more godly than we really are, the Bible calls it hypocrisy. When we pretend to look different physically than we really are, the Bible calls it vanity. In the aforementioned sermon, Wesley continued, "The wearing of flamboyant or costly apparel naturally tends to breed and to increase vanity. By vanity, I mean the love and desire of being admired and praised. Every one of you that is fond of dress has a witness of this in your own heart. You know in your hearts it is with a view to be admired that you so adorn yourselves. You know that you would not take the same pains if no one was to see you but God and His holy angels. Now, the more you indulge this foolish desire, the more it grows upon you. You have vanity enough by nature; but by thus indulging it, you increase it a hundred-fold. Aim at pleasing God, and these ornaments will disappear."[41]

Wasting God's Money

Luke and Lydia Lovejoy also realize that part of the bigger picture is the waste of God's money. It was the rich man "who was clothed in purple and fine linen" and refused to help the beggar Lazarus (Luke 16:19). The Lovejoys can't imagine Jesus decking Himself out in expensive clothing or decorating His body with gold and jewels. He would have been adorning Himself with food taken from the mouths of the hungry. Lydia recently read that women spend an enormous $426 billion every year on beauty products.[42] "Think what could be done with that money for the poor!" she exclaims.

And that's merely what women spend on cosmetics and other beauty products. When we add what both men and women spend on expensive and fashionable clothing, the overall sum is staggering. Wesley pointed out, "Every shilling which you save from your own clothing, you may expend in clothing the naked and relieving the various necessities of the poor. Therefore, every shilling which you needlessly spend on your apparel is, in effect, stolen from God and from the poor! For what purpose did you buy these ornaments? To please God? No, but to please your own fancy or to gain the admiration and applause of those that were no wiser than yourself."[43]

Luke Lovejoy's Application

Lydia Lovejoy has enthusiastically embraced these teachings on adornment, but what about her husband Luke? Unlike some men, Luke doesn't take the position that since both Peter and Paul address their commandments to women, he can simply ignore them. After examining the reasons behind the commandments, he sees that the same principles apply equally to men and women. If it's wrong for a woman to put on an artificial exterior, it's wrong for a man to do so. If women are to dress modestly, so are men. Vanity is vanity and artificiality is artificiality, whether it's in a man or a woman. Luke knows that wasting money on expensive clothing is no different for a man than it is for a woman.

Both Luke and Lydia know that when God gave us these commands about adornment and clothing, He wasn't trying to add an additional burden to our lives. He is trying to shape our souls to make them as beautiful as possible. When we realize this, it's not only easy to obey these commands, but it's also easy to *love* them.

In the next section, we're going to look at some of the provisions God has made to help us live the Kingdom Life.

HELPS TO LIVING THE KINGDOM LIFE

23

Bible Study and Reflection

If you would follow on to know the Lord, come at once to the open Bible expecting it to speak to you. Do not come with the notion that it is a thing which you may push around at your convenience. –A. W. Tozer

Nothing is so likely a means to fill us with Christ's spirit and dispositions, as to be frequent in reading the Gospels. For they contain the history of His life and behavior in the world. –William Law

J. C. Ryle said, "Next to praying there is nothing so important in practical religion as Bible-reading."[44] He spoke wisely, for one of the primary ways Gods speaks to us today is through our reading and meditating on the Scriptures. Matthew Henry writes, "God has something to say to us as a friend every day by the written Word, in which we must hear His voice."

Reading the Scriptures is the most accurate way to consult the mind of God. Counsel from other Christians may be in error. Subjective feelings can easily be our own imaginations, rather than God speaking to us. However, when we read the Scriptures, we know God Himself is speaking to us with infallible words.

Tozer observed, "God did not write a book and send it by a messenger to be read at a distance by unaided minds. He spoke a Book and lives in His spoken words, constantly speaking His words and causing the power of them to persist across the years."[45] So when we read the Bible, we should approach it as a book that is *now* speaking to us—not something that was once spoken and is now only history.

Reading Daily

As we've discussed, we should read the Scriptures daily as part of our devotional time. Those who live the Kingdom Life would never think of letting a day pass without praying to God. They should likewise never let a day pass without letting God speak to them through His Word. Committed Christians often look to the Bereans as an example in Bible reading—and rightfully so. Have you ever noticed how often the Bereans searched the Scriptures? The account says they "searched the Scriptures *daily* to find out whether these things were so" (Acts 17:11).

Jesus pointed to the essential nourishment from Scripture when He said, "Man shall not live by bread alone, but by every word that proceeds from the mouth of God" (Matt. 4:4). Have you ever thought about the Bible that way—as something essential to life? Do you nourish your soul on Scripture each day, the way you nourish your body with food?

One secret of the Kingdom Life is to develop the habit of reading God's Word every day. It needs to be as much a part of our daily routine as eating, dressing, washing, and sleeping. I've suggested that you make it part of your devotional hour with God. However, it may work better for you to read the Scriptures at some other time.

At first, you may find reading the Bible a drudgery that you can't wait to get over with. You may have to force yourself to stick to a regular reading schedule. However, unless there is something in your life impeding the Holy Spirit, you will eventually find incredible joy in reading the Scriptures. You'll find you can't wait to find out what new thing you will discover each day in Scripture. I don't mean you'll find a new theological doctrine, but rather a new understanding or conviction that had previously escaped your notice. You'll be like someone who has read midway through a mystery novel and looks forward to every opportunity to pick up the novel and continue reading.

Cherishing the Bible

When you embark on your daily Bible reading, don't approach the Scriptures as dry, dusty tomes. Rather, read the Bible the way a young adult reads a cherished love letter. I realize that in today's world, letters have been largely replaced by e-mails, tweets, and text messages. Nevertheless, picture a young man from another era as he anxiously waits for the mail each day, hoping it will contain a letter from his beloved. When he goes to his mailbox and finds the expected letter, his eyes widen as he rips open the envelope. He devours the letter, whispering each word aloud as he reads.

He's not satisfied to read it just once. The first day he carries it with him as he travels to work. On the bus, he pulls it out and reads it again. He smiles as he reads over special parts. Throughout the day, he carries the letter next to his heart and ponders some of the things his beloved has said. He reads it again on the bus ride home and thinks about it as he lies in bed that night.[46]

That is exactly how we should read the Bible—as a letter from our Beloved. God's Word gives us precious insight into His nature and character. Through the pages of Scripture, God tells us how much He loves us. He also gives us exciting insights into the invisible realm of heaven and the angels. He warns us of spiritual dangers. He sets forth our rights, privileges, and responsibilities as citizens of His kingdom. He points out who and what our enemies are and how we can defeat them. Finally, He clarifies what we must do if we are to spend eternity with Him.

So when we read the Scriptures, we might want to imagine ourselves sitting at the feet of Jesus or one of the apostles or prophets, learning from them and drinking in what they have to say. Before reading, we should ask God to help the pages of Scripture become alive to us.

Reading for Spiritual Nourishment

Many Christians read the Bible primarily for head knowledge. They have a long list of carefully worked out theological doctrines, for which they seek reinforcement every time they read the Scriptures. They have memorized an assemblage of selectively chosen proof texts for their positions, with which they'll bombard anyone who dares to challenge their theological fortress. Such people acquire masses of knowledge each time they read Scripture, but little spiritual nourishment. Despite all their learning, they know little about the Kingdom Life. This is not surprising, for those very same Scriptures tell us, "Knowledge puffs up, but love edifies" (1 Cor. 8:1).

Therefore, if you're seeking the Kingdom Life don't read the Bible primarily for head knowledge. Read it for spiritual sustenance and life. Read to learn what kind of person God wants us to be. Hear our God of love speak to you. Learn from Him how to grow in His image. Learn about the fruit He requires and how to produce it. Read with attention and reverence to learn how to live the Kingdom Life.

Remember that the Scriptures were given to us for "instruction in righteousness" (2 Tim. 3:16). So we should use the Scriptures as a mirror to measure our own lives and our growth in Christ. William Law said this about the Bible writers: "Receive their sacred words with as much attention and reverence as if you saw their persons, and knew that they had just come from heaven on purpose to teach you the way that leads to heaven."[47]

Pondering the Scriptures

As we read, we can each ask ourselves, "What do these words mean in *my* life? How does God want me to live? How can I constantly enjoy His favor? What spiritual dangers is God warning me about? What are my privileges and responsibilities as a Christian?" As we've already discussed, when we read God's Word we should also be constantly praying—praising God, confessing disobedience in our lives concerning the things we read, making commitments to live by what we're reading, and asking for power to live by the teachings He is giving us that day through the Scriptures.

The commitments we make to God as we read should be more than just general resolutions. Instead, we should make them very specific: "Father, I resolve with your help to quit allowing myself to become angry at Pete's rude behavior at work." Or, "Father, I've been harboring resentment toward Susan for years because of the hurt she caused me. I confess this and I hereby forgive her. And I resolve, with your power, to bury this matter permanently."

William Law writes, "When men retire into their studies to change their nature, to correct and reform their passions, to find out the folly and weakness of their hearts, when they read and meditate to fill their souls with spiritual wisdom and to raise their hearts unto God—when this is learning, then learning will lead men unto God."[48]

In chapter 8 we talked about the Victorious Cycle and the necessary interaction among prayer, obedience, and faith. We now need to insert Bible reading into that cycle. How can we obey Christ if we don't know what His commands are? Bible reading enables us to know how to live, which in turn makes our prayers more effective.

Stripping Away Our Blinders

Sadly, many—if not most—Christians miss the rich spiritual treasure they can find in the Scriptures. Why? Because they read the Bible with blinders on. The blinders are our preconceptions. Most of us have already been thoroughly indoctrinated in "what the Bible teaches" long before we ever read the Scriptures for ourselves. So when we read the pages of Scripture, instead of hearing God speak, we typically hear the indoctrination given by our instructors.

So here is another secret of the Kingdom Life: in order to hear God speak to us through the Scriptures, it's essential that we read the Bible with a blank slate. But how can we do that since we've all been indoctrinated in various ways? The way to get past our preconceptions is to read the Bible as would a new Christian who has not yet been taught any of the "truths" of Christianity. This untainted Christian reads the Scriptures without any previous knowledge of what they say. He has nothing to prove. And he has nothing to defend.

Of course, few of us are such untainted Christians. So when we read, each of us should ask the question, "If I didn't know 'better,' what would I think this passage is saying?" Jesus told us, "Whoever does not receive the kingdom of God as a little child will by no means enter it" (Mark 10:15). So read the Scriptures as a little child, taking Scripture at face value. Unless you're reading an apocalyptic book or an obviously highly figurative passage, assume the passage means exactly what it says—regardless of whose theology it steps on. Not that you're reading for theology. However, when you read with a blank slate, you can't help but notice that today's theology of easy believism negates many of the commands and other teachings of Scripture.

As you read through Scripture—particularly the New Testament—make a list of all of the commandments, instructions, and insights on the Christian life. Assume those passages mean just what they say. Go back over each commandment or instruction and ask yourself, "What is the purpose of this command? Why did God give it? What does this tell me about the character of God?" Sometimes the surrounding verses will provide some clarification. Other times you will simply have to prayerfully reflect on the matter. The important thing is to *obey* it, regardless of whether you understand God's purpose behind it. However, reflecting on the purpose of the commandment is one of the things that sets apart those who live the Kingdom Life.

When you read the Bible in this manner, you are certain to come across new truths and teachings you never noticed before. I'm sure I have read most New Testament passages at least a thousand times throughout my lifetime. Yet every day when I read Scripture, I notice something new that has escaped me before. I don't mean that the actual words on the page have escaped me. Rather, the significance of certain statements has. Read the Bible expecting to find new blessings every day!

Removing the Human Influence

When we read the Scriptures, we should be reading because we want to hear the words of God, not the words of man. But learning to set aside our indoctrination and preconceptions is only one step in removing the human element. The truth is that man's fallible influence is on every page of our Bibles, even though most of us don't realize it.

"How?" you might be asking. "I don't use a study Bible. I just read the Word of God itself."

But do you? I assume the Bible you read is divided into chapters, paragraphs, and verses. All those divisions are manmade. God didn't give us His Word partitioned, crisscrossed, subdivided, and demarcated. Each book of the Bible (except the Psalms) came as a packaged whole, without any paragraphs, subheadings, chapters, verses, or other subdivisions. Stephen Langton, Roman Catholic Archbishop of Canterbury, created our New Testament chapter divisions in the year 1227. Robert Stephanus divided those New Testament chapters into verses in 1555. The subheadings and paragraphs came even later. They're usually added by the modern translators or publishers.

Many Christians think they're imitating the Bereans when they look up all the Bible citations given by a speaker or writer. However, when the Bereans checked Paul's teaching, they had no chapters or verses in their Bibles. They had to read through an entire Bible book (or scroll) to find out if what Paul was saying was true. This meant they were forced to take notice of the context of the passages they were reading.

Chapter and verse designations are handy for cross-reference. However, these subdivisions heavily influence how we understand the Bible. For example, most Christians mistakenly think the passage in the New Testament concerning the head covering (1 Cor. 11:1-16) pertains to conduct in church. However, nothing in that passage limits the instructions to church services. The reason so many Christians imagine the covering applies only to church is that in our Bibles the passage on head coverings is grouped with Paul's discussion of the Lord's Supper (1 Cor. 11:17-34), and the two are combined into a single chapter. Since the Lord's Supper concerns church conduct, the reader is naturally drawn to the conclusion that the instructions on head coverings pertain to church conduct.

Chapter ten of First Corinthians pertains to everyday meals and other matters outside of church services. So if Archbishop Langton had included the head covering instructions in chapter ten, most readers would no doubt assume that the instructions on head coverings apply in all situations. In short, the chapter and verse divisions sometimes influence how we interpret Scripture.

Ignoring Chapters and Verses

Therefore, when you read the New Testament, I encourage you to read an entire book in one sitting. This is achievable with most of the epistles. As you read, ignore all subheadings, paragraphs, and chapter and verse divisions. Instead, carefully follow the line of thought from sentence to sentence. Often the first part of one chapter belongs to the last part of the preceding chapter. Ignoring the chapter divisions allows you to read the epistle as an entire, unified message—as God intended it to be read.

I realize that you probably will not have time to read the larger New Testament books in one sitting. The same is true of most Old Testament books. So with the larger books, try at least to read an entire block of related chapters together. For example, read the entire Sermon on the Mount in one sitting. Similarly, when reading the Gospel of John, try to read the entire account of the Last Supper (John 13 through 17) in a single reading.

If you're using a study Bible, ignore all human interpretative commentary. At the same time, some study material is very helpful—such as cross-references, maps, and explanatory notes on money and units of measurement. Translator's notes are helpful when they explain to the reader that a given phrase or word can be translated in more than one way. Such translator's notes help put us on the same level as the original New Testament audience.

The other human factor we want to remove is our own flesh. The New Testament contains many commandments and instructions that require denying ourselves and carrying our cross. To those not living the Kingdom Life, such commandments may appear to be heavy, oppressive burdens. So the human tendency is either to ignore them or to explain them away as we read. More than likely, others have already explained them away for us, making it easy to simply read their adulterations into the text.

However, when we live the Kingdom Life, we *want* to know what God requires of us. As we've discussed, we know He gives directives because He loves us and wants to gently mold us into the image of His Son. So we don't want to find a way *around* God's laws. Rather, we want to embrace them as fully as possible. We look at the Bible and its commandments as a blessed help to living the Kingdom Life.

Now let's look at another help God has given us—the church.

24

Accountability to the Church

Surrendered Christians anchor their work to the local church. –William MacDonald

Our own devout life will be greatly helped by association with other devout souls. –Francis of Sales

In parts of the northern wilds of Canada's subarctic plains, wolves still hunt American buffalo. Adult buffalo weigh ten to twenty times as much as the wolves who hunt them, and with their large, sharp horns, these buffalo make formidable foes. In fact, as long as the buffalo stand their ground and stay together in a herd, it's almost impossible for the wolves to kill any of them.

So the tactic of the wolves is to harass the buffalo until the herd gets spooked and begins to run. The wolves then chase the buffalo herd for miles with a sole purpose in mind: to isolate one single buffalo, usually a calf or a sick animal. Once they succeed in isolating one of the buffalo, the wolves then go in for the kill.

Satan uses the same tactic in bringing down Christians—isolate us and then destroy us spiritually. As the Scriptures say, "A man who isolates himself seeks his own desire; he rages against all wise judgment" (Prov. 18:1). The Kingdom Life can't be lived in isolation from other Christians, unless it's the isolation of prison during persecution. We can't surrender our lives to Christ if we can't surrender ourselves to His church. That's because the church is His body. Those who live the Kingdom Life are active members of a local congregation of believers, particularly a congregation where there is a high degree of accountability among all.

One of the reasons Christ gave us the Church is so Christians can help one another in the Christian life. John Wesley made this comment: "This was the original design of the Church of Christ. It is a body of men compacted together, in order, first, to save each his own soul; then to assist each other in working out their salvation. They are united together to oppose the devil and all his works, and to wage war against the world and the flesh, his constant and faithful allies."[49]

This is what the local church is supposed to be—a band of brothers and sisters working together to "fight the good fight" and watch over each other in love. United we stand; divided we fall. This is how groups like the early Christians, the Waldensians, and the Anabaptists faithfully endured centuries of persecution. In fact, they didn't just *endure* such persecution, they *prospered* under it. Accountability to each other proved to be the key.

What the Scriptures Teach About Accountability

The majority of Christians today think that their spiritual condition is their own private affair. They think they only have to answer to Christ and nobody else. However, the Scriptures teach the exact opposite. In his first letter to the Corinthians, Paul explains how the body of Christ works:

> But now indeed there are many members, yet one body. And the eye cannot say to the hand, "I have no need of you"; nor again the head to the feet, "I have no need of you." No, much rather, those members of the body which seem to be weaker are necessary. . .that there should be no schism in the

> body, but that the members should have the same care for one another. And if one member suffers, all the members suffer with it; or if one member is honored, all the members rejoice with it. Now you are the body of Christ, and members individually.
> 1 Cor. 12:20-27

Is Your Left Foot Independent?

Following Paul's analogy, imagine if you were walking barefoot and you stepped on some broken glass with your left foot. Would that be the concern of your left foot alone? Not at all. The pain would shoot through the rest of your body. You would no doubt instantly bend down and pull any bits of glass out of your foot. The left foot couldn't say, "Hey, if I want to go around with pieces of glass in me that's no concern to the rest of the body."

But pain isn't the only issue. The entire body could theoretically bleed to death from a cut on the foot if the body had no mechanisms to stop the flow of blood. The blood that flows through your left foot circulates throughout your body. In fact before you ever stepped on the glass, your body had been manufacturing clotting factors and platelets so it would be prepared to stop any bleeding. So when your left foot stepped on the glass, platelets immediately formed a plug at the site of the injury. Then clotting factors almost instantly formed protein strands called fibrin to strengthen the plug. Your left foot had no say in any of this. The rest of the body took these actions to protect itself.

But there are even more issues here. Bacteria and other pathogens have likely entered the blood stream through the cuts in your left foot. This presents danger of infection to your whole body, not just your left foot. So our whole body will fight the potential infection with many different parts of our immune system. Specially designed antibodies will attack specific types of bacteria and other pathogens. Again, your left foot has no say in any of this.

Our Spiritual Health

Just like the health and well-being of a person's left foot is the concern of the whole body, so likewise a person's spiritual health concerns the local congregation to which he belongs. It's not just his concern. If he becomes spiritually infected, his infection could spread to other members of the local body. As Paul asked the Corinthians, "Do you not know that a little leaven leavens the whole lump?" (1 Cor. 5:6).

Furthermore, our church leaders are concerned about our personal spiritual well-being, not just that of the congregation as a whole. That's why the Scriptures tell us, "Obey those who rule over you, and be submissive, for they watch out for your souls, as those who must give account. Let them do so with joy and not with grief, for that would be unprofitable for you" (Heb. 13:17). When we live the Kingdom Life, we *welcome* the fact that others are watching over our souls. We do what we can to make their task a joyous one.

Mutual Accountability

Through the centuries, one of the greatest helps to Christians living the Kingdom Life has been to be part of a church or spiritual society where there is mutual accountability, one to another. Such churches have made it easier for their members to obey Christ's commands by maintaining supportive biblical standards.

25

How Church Standards Can Help

This is liberty, true gospel liberty, experienced by every believer: Not freedom from the law of God, or the works of God, but from the law of sin and the works of the devil. –John Wesley

The two things which, of all others, need the most to be under a strict rule are our time and our money. –William Law

Church standards or rules of conduct can be an enormous help in our quest for obedience. My dictionary defines *standards* as "those morals, ethics, and habits established by authority, custom, or an individual as acceptable."[50] Just as it is with plain dress, most people today associate church standards with the so-called "plain churches"—conservative Amish, Mennonite, and Brethren churches. However, church standards have been around since the days of the early church.

Early Christian congregations often used manuals of church life. The *Didache* is the earliest of these surviving manuals, and it dates back to about the year 100. Some other surviving church manuals are the *Apostolic Tradition of Hippolytus* (c. 200), the *Didascalia* (c. 250), and the *Apostolic Constitutions* (c. 390).

These church manuals make specific applications of various New Testament principles of conduct. For example, most of them list specific occupations from which Christians were excluded, such as actors, magicians, and gladiators. Of course, none of these church manuals were intended to cover every type of sin. Instead, they focused on the most prevalent issues of their day. By their very nature, manuals for Christian living can't adequately cover what Jesus called the weightier matters—justice, mercy, and faith. Nor can they enforce the two greatest commandments: to love God with our whole heart, soul, mind, and strength, and to love our neighbor as ourselves.

After AD 400, church manuals largely fell into disuse. Thereafter, church discipline mainly depended on the zeal and concern of the local bishop. Nevertheless, Christians who were serious about their Christian walk often voluntarily put themselves under the rule of life of some Christian community. During the Middle Ages, these communities were nearly always limited to single, celibate Christians. Married Christians and those who didn't want to join a community had to develop their own personal rules of life based on the teachings of Scripture.

Most of the groups who broke from the Catholic Church during the Middle Ages—such as the Lollards, Waldensians, and Czech Brethren—featured strong church standards that distinguished their lives from their Catholic neighbors. In fact, during the Middle Ages, the authorities often suspected as heretics those who were living exceptionally godly lives.

After the Reformation, some churches reinstituted church standards or rules of conduct for their members. The most notable of these were the Anabaptist, Moravian, and Calvinist churches. Over time other churches made use of church standards, such as the Quakers, the English Baptists, and the German Baptist Brethren. In addition to such churches, numerous spiritual societies—both large and small—flourished inside the larger state churches, such as the Roman Catholic, Anglican, and Lutheran churches. The most famous of these societies were the Methodist Societies founded by John and Charles Wesley.

The Methodist Societies

John Wesley was one of the most effective evangelists of all time. He preached over 42,000 sermons throughout his life and was instrumental in the conversion of tens of thousands of people. However, Wesley never founded a church. The Methodist church was not established until after he died. Rather than starting a church, Wesley tried to support the existing churches.

At the same time, Wesley organized hundreds of Methodist societies. These societies were companies of people who met weekly for Bible study, prayer, and mutual encouragement. They lived by a list of standards that comprised a rule of life. People who didn't live by the society's standards were soon excluded from the group. The Methodist societies met on evenings when there was no church service, so as not to compete with the local churches. Many of Wesley's converts joined one of these Methodist societies, but many did not. Several years into his ministry, Wesley made this observation:

> The far greater part of those who had begun to "fear God and work righteousness," but were not united together in a society, grew faint in their minds and within a few months fell back into what they were before. Meanwhile the far greater part of those who were thus united together continued "striving to enter in at the strait gate," and to "lay hold on eternal life." They wanted to "flee from the wrath to come," and to assist each other in so doing. They therefore united themselves in order to pray together, to receive the word of exhortation, and to watch over one another in love, that they might help each other to "work out their salvation."[51]

Wesley discovered that disciplinary standards, joined with prayer and teaching, make an enormous difference as to whether someone stays on the Vine and produces fruit or else falls by the wayside.

The Methodist Standards

The rule of life for the Methodist societies addressed both negative and positive conduct. In other words, their standards set forth things the members were to *avoid*, and they set forth things the members were to *do*:

First: By doing no harm, by avoiding evil of every kind, especially that which is most generally practiced, such as:

- taking of the name of God in vain;
- profaning the day of the Lord, either by doing ordinary work therein or by buying or selling;
- drunkenness: buying or selling spirituous liquors, or drinking them, unless in cases of extreme necessity;
- slaveholding; buying or selling slaves;
- fighting, quarreling, brawling, brother going to law with brother;
- returning evil for evil, or railing for railing;
- using many words in buying or selling [i.e., haggling];
- buying or selling smuggled goods
- giving or taking things on usury
- uncharitable or unprofitable conversation; particularly speaking evil of magistrates or of ministers;
- doing to others as we would not want them to do unto us;

- doing what we know is not for the glory of God, such as the "putting on of gold and costly apparel;"
- Engaging in such amusements as cannot rightly be done in the name of the Lord Jesus;
- singing such songs or reading such books that do not tend to the knowledge or love of God;
- luxury and needless self-indulgence;
- laying up treasure upon earth;
- borrowing without a probability of paying; or purchasing goods on credit without a probability of paying for them.

Secondly, It is expected of all who remain in these societies that they should continue to evidence their desire of salvation by doing good:

- by being in every way merciful according to their power;
- as they have opportunity, doing good of every possible sort and as far as possible to all men—to their bodies, according to the ability that God gives, by giving food to the hungry, by clothing the naked, and by visiting or helping those who are sick or in prison;
- to their souls, by instructing, reproving, or exhorting all whom we have any dealing with.

By doing good, especially to those who are of the household of faith or seeking to be so:

- by employing them preferably to others;
- by buying from one another, helping each other in business, and so much more because the world will love its own and only its own;

- by living with all possible diligence and frugality, so that the gospel is not reproached;
- by running with patience the race that is set before us, "denying ourselves, and taking up our cross daily;"
- by willingly bearing the reproach of Christ, to be as the filth and offscouring of the world;
- by expecting that men will say all manner of evil about us falsely, for the Lord's sake.

Thirdly, It is expected of all who desire to remain in these societies that they should continue to demonstrate their desire of salvation by attending upon all the ordinances of God, such as:

- the public worship of God;
- the ministry of the Word, read or expounded;
- the Supper of the Lord;
- family and private prayer;
- searching the Scriptures;
- fasting or abstinence.[52]

Some Christians mistakenly think it is "unspiritual" to be subject to church standards. Yet such standards were the key to the spirituality of the original Methodist societies—as well as to many other Christian movements. In fact, virtually all of the great spiritual classics were penned by Christians who belonged to a church, society, or Christian community with a rule of life.

Nevertheless, as helpful as church standards are, they do have their limitations, as we're about to see.

26

The Limitations of Church Standards

Church or society standards normally work for the spiritual good of those who live by them. However, some Christians limit their obedience only to those things that are in the standards of their church or society. This may not sound so bad at first. However, the problem is that church standards inherently bear four important limitations:

1. They rarely cover *all* of God's commandments. In fact, most rules of life don't purport to do so. As a result, a person can live by all the standards established by a church or society and yet be disobedient to Christ. For example, as beneficial and comprehensive as was the Methodist rule of life, it contained some glaring omissions. Nothing is said in it about going to war, taking oaths, or head coverings (Matt. 5:33-48; 1 Cor. 11:1-16).

2. Standards and rules of life primarily address *external* conduct. By their very nature, church standards focus on obedience to the outward commandments of Scripture. However, when Jesus spoke of the "weightier matters of the law," He named justice, mercy, and faith. And, of course, love is even weightier than those three. Yet these are qualities and characteristics of the heart, which are not easily defined or regulated by standards. Church standards can control our outward conduct, but only God can see what's in our hearts. So we should never imagine that our standing with God is assured just because we comply with our church's standards.

3. Standards tend to become lax over time. Religious movements tend to lose their initial fervor as time passes. As movements or churches lose their first love, members typically make their standards more permissive. Or else they ignore their standards altogether. The Methodist societies never watered down the original standards set forth by John Wesley. But over time they simply ignored them.

4. Church standards are often related to the time period in which they were written. Rules of life and church standards understandably address issues that are relevant at the time they're written. For example, the *Apostolic Tradition of Hippolytus* denies baptism to charioteers and gladiators. Those were important issues in AD 200. But they're non-issues in the twenty-first century.

The rule of life of the Methodist societies forbids "buying or selling smuggled goods." Although that rule would still be applicable today, it's rarely an issue for most of us. However, in eighteenth-century England and its colonies, buying smuggled goods was a huge issue. On the other hand, the Methodist rule of life addresses neither abortion nor divorce. That's because abortion was illegal in eighteenth century England and divorce was extremely rare.

Sometimes church standards can continue a life of their own long after the original intent has become obsolete. A classic example is one of the original rules of the Quakers (Society of Friends), instituted by their founder George Fox. Their standards required members to use the word *thee* when addressing other people, regardless of their class. At the time George Fox instituted this rule, people in his region of England used the pronoun *thee* when addressing equals or inferiors. They reserved use of the pronoun *you* for addressing their superiors. Since there should be no class distinctions among Christians, Fox insisted that his followers use the word *thee* when addressing everyone, regardless of class.

That standard made sense at the time it was instituted. However, less than a century after George Fox made this rule, the distinction between *thee* and *you* disappeared in English society. People began to use *you* when addressing everyone, regardless of class. *Thee* became an obsolete word. Yet rather than acknowledging the fact that the pronoun *you* now applied to all classes, Quakers continued to use *thee* as if the word *you* was still used only for superiors. What the Quakers called "plain language" had actually become quaint or obsolete language. To this day, some Quakers still use *thee* when addressing fellow Quakers.

So if a church or organization wants its standards to stay spiritually meaningful, it must be diligent to keep them updated. By "updated" I do not mean that a church should modify its standards to fit the ever-changing dictates of the world. Rather, I mean that standards concerning issues that no longer exist should be deleted. Also, a church should add new standards to fit new challenges.

Ichabod and Lucretia

Ichabod and Lucretia Yoder are members of a "plain" church, and they scrupulously follow all their church's standards. Ichabod wears a black hat and the prescribed men's clothing, and Lucretia wears a cape dress and head covering. They avoid all the forms of worldly entertainment prohibited by their church. To most of the people in their church, they appear model Christians.

However, their personal spiritual life is almost nonexistent. Although they regularly attend their church's prayer meetings, neither of them prays alone very often. Nor do they read the Scriptures at home. In fact, both Ichabod and Lucretia prefer secular books to Christian books. Although Lucretia wears a very conspicuous head covering, she is anything but submissive to her husband. She frequently bosses him around and scolds him. He, in turn, does not treat her very lovingly. Yet none of these things violate any specific standards of their church, so neither of them think much about it.

Ichabod and Lucretia hold grudges against several families in the church, and they are the source of much of the church's gossip. Although they wear plain clothes, their lifestyle is actually rather expensive. They drive a late-model Mercedes Benz—black, so it doesn't violate their church's standards. Although they already live in an expensive home, they are constantly remodeling and improving it with trendy upgrades and interior designs.

Some people might assume they're living the Kingdom Life. The truth is that their hearts are far from the kingdom of God. However, no one suspects this—nor do they themselves realize it. That's because they perfectly obey their church's standards. They have an obedient relationship with their church, but not an intimate relationship with Christ.

It's not for me to say where the Yoders will stand on Judgment Day. However, I can say that they are not living the Kingdom Life. They are not where Christ wants them to be. Obedience to godly church standards is far better than no obedience. But Christ calls us to something even greater.

How to Avoid Being Like the Yoders

I want to make absolutely clear that my analysis of the Yoders is in no way a criticism of biblical church standards. I myself belong to a plain congregation with church standards. The problem isn't church standards. The problem is Christians who ignore Scriptural commands just because those commands aren't part of their church standards. For those of us who belong to congregations with church standards, how do we avoid ending up like the Yoders?

The starting point is to recognize that although the church exists as an essential and integral part of the Christian life, our primary relationship and loyalty is to Christ Himself. We should have a healthy, supportive, and submissive relationship with our church, but we need an even stronger obedient faith-love relationship with Christ.

No church can create our inner life for us. No church can keep watch on us around the clock. We have to develop our inner spiritual life personally, between us and God. We also have to consciously live in His presence, for He is both watching us and guarding us every minute of the day. Those of us who belong to a church with standards must always keep in mind that no church's standards can cover every commandment given by God or every situation that arises in life. We should view our church's standards as the *minimum* level of Christian conduct.

So in addition to their church's standards, Christians who live the Kingdom Life should have their own personal rules of life based on *all* the teachings of Scripture. Church standards don't usually cover our prayer and devotional life, but our personal rule of life should. Our personal rule of life should particularly include those weightier—but inner—matters such as love, mercy, and kindness.

When I say that each of us should have our own rule of life, I don't mean that we should become individualists. Nor do I mean that we should have a holier-than-thou attitude among our brethren. I simply mean that our sights should be fixed on the commands of God. Just because our church hasn't formally addressed a particular New Testament teaching in its standards doesn't mean we are free to ignore it.

When our compass is set on the Bible as our ultimate standard, then our conduct doesn't change just because our church decides to lower some of its standards. Godly church standards are an enormous aid in the Christian walk, but they can never replace a close, obedient love-faith relationship with Jesus Christ. Still we can be thankful to have such supportive church standards.

Further Blessings from the Church

Up to this point, we've talked about how Christ gave us His church to assist us in living the Christian life. Some of the ways churches help us is through pastoral shepherding, mutual accountability, and church standards. Another way the church helps us is through its weekly services. So now let's talk about how we can get the maximum benefit out of our church's services.

27

Getting the Most Out of Church Services

God is more glorified when we unite with our brethren and join our praise offerings to theirs. –Francis of Sales

If we want Jesus to go with us to the meeting, we must invite Him home with us after the meeting. –Samuel Logan Brengle

Those living the Kingdom Life aren't satisfied to just show up each Sunday and warm a church pew. They look forward to the weekly church meetings as high points of their Christian walk. However, what we get out of our church services depends to a large degree on what we put into them.

Preparation

First of all, we should prepare for each meeting to the extent we're able. If the service will include a Sunday school lesson or Bible study, we should study the material ahead of time. This will enable us to meaningfully participate in the discussion or to follow it with understanding. If the church will be asking for prayer requests, we should come with prayer requests in mind. If our church provides a time for members to share testimonies about their week, we should come prepared to share a meaningful testimony when possible. Also, we should pray throughout the week for those who will be teaching and preaching during the coming church meetings.

Adequate Sleep

A second but equally important way to prepare for the Sunday morning meeting is to get sufficient rest during the week. Through the prophet Malachi, God denounced the unfaithful Israelites who offered up blind, lame, and blemished animals for sacrifice, saying, "When you offer the lame and sick, is it not evil?" (Mal. 1:8). Of course it's evil. Yet that is exactly what so many Christians do today.

True, we don't bring animal sacrifices to the house of God. But we are supposed to offer up our "bodies a living sacrifice, holy, acceptable to God" (Rom. 12:1). What kind of body do we offer up to God on Sunday morning? Many Christians push themselves so hard during the week that they neglect their sleep. Then on Sunday they drag themselves to church and offer to God whatever they have left over—which often isn't much. As a result, they either sleep or fight sleep for most of the service, struggling to be mentally engaged in the teaching and worship.

God offered the following challenge to the unfaithful Israelites about their blemished sacrifices: "Offer it then to your governor! Would he be pleased with you?" (Mal. 1:8). We can ask the same question today. Would we drag a tired, sleepy body to work and offer it to our employer on Monday morning? Would we dare to sleep on our job or at our business?

If our employers or customers wouldn't accept such an offering, why do we imagine that God does? If we see that we are worn out and sleepy Sunday after Sunday, then we need to make some serious adjustments in our work or recreation schedules. We should offer to God our very best on Sunday mornings—not what's left over after we've given our best for mammon.

Go to Church With a Prayerful Spirit

Pray before leaving your house to attend a church meeting. Ask God to bless the meeting and to be with the pastor and with all those who will speak and teach. Also ask God to accompany you to church and help you be alert and attentive throughout the service. Pray that God will speak to you personally through the sermon, devotionals, comments, and lessons.

Just as we maintain continual communion with God throughout the week, we should do so throughout the service. "Father, help this speaker to present his ideas clearly." "Father help me to see how this lesson applies in my life." "Father, help me to put this into practice." "Father, help all of us to be attentive during this sermon." With practice we can make the entire service a continuous chain of short prayers.

Be an Encourager!

When the service is over, look for opportunities to be a source of encouragement to your brothers and sisters. Seek out the ones who spoke or taught during that service and let them know you appreciated what they shared. Before you approach them, try to have one or more specific points in mind that blessed you.

When conversing with others, ask how their week went. Commiserate with those who have had struggles or sickness. Gather prayer requests as you talk. But don't entrust these requests to your memory. Rather, always have a small notebook with you so that you can write down such requests on the spot. This will let your brother know you're serious about praying for him. Also, this will ensure you won't forget to intercede for them during the coming week. Likewise, share your prayer needs with others. Finally, make it your aim that all of your conversations after church will be upbuilding to others.

Returning Home from Church

Finally, bring Jesus home with you. That is, don't let church end when you get into your vehicle to go home. As you return home, maintain the same prayerful spirit you had before and during the service. Imagine that Jesus is a passenger in your car—because He is.

Nothing destroys the benefits of a church service faster than to let a carnal, complaining spirit take over as you begin to drive home. Let's listen in on the conversation of Bill and Patsy Complainer as they return from church.

Bill and Patsy Complainer

"Oh, was that sermon ever boring!" Bill grumbled as he drove out of the church parking lot. "I thought it would never end."

"Yeah," Patsy chimed in. "Not only that, but Brother Isaac didn't seem very well prepared for his Sunday school lesson, did he? I didn't get a thing out of it."

"Me neither," Bill concurred. "Did you notice how bratty little Sammy Miller was? Are his parents blind to how he behaves in church? That boy needs some discipline."

"It's unbelievable how some parents are so oblivious to their children's behavior," Patsy added. "By the way, did you notice who came in late as usual?"

Does that sound typical? Hopefully not. However, in too many vehicles that's the type of conversation going on as a family drives home from church. In a few minutes they've totally erased any spiritual benefit they obtained from the service. If you find that you've fallen into such a rut of complaining, try imitating the conversation of Bob and Meg Grateful as they drive home from church.

Bob and Meg Grateful

"Did you catch that point about reaching out to our neighbors in Brother Mel's sermon?" Bob asked.

"Yes. I thought he made some excellent suggestions there," Meg replied. "Let's try to put some of them into practice this week."

"I agree. I've certainly been weak in that area. And what did you think about Sunday school? Wasn't that interesting about who the Philistines were?"

"That was a new one for me," Meg answered. "I appreciate the research Brother Conrad put into his lesson. I never realized that the name Palestine came from the Philistines."

"Oh, by the way," Bob interjected, "we need to be praying for John Rockford. He mentioned to me after church that there's a possibility he might get laid off from his job."

"Definitely," Meg agreed. "And Rosemary Martin has a medical checkup this week that she's pretty concerned about."

Bringing Jesus Home With Us

Yes, we can either bring the prayerful spirit of church home with us, or we can immediately drown it out with complaining and other negative talk. This isn't to say that we can never say anything unfavorable about church. There may be actual defects that need to be remedied. Such matters should be brought up tactfully to the church leadership. However, we don't have to let such issues turn us into habitual complainers.

Nineteenth-century pastor Samuel Logan Brendle made this observation: "Jesus will not come to the meeting and return with us to our door, if when we get home we find it in our hearts to bid Him good day and close the door in His face. And then we go in and scold the wife and children and talk about our neighbors and forget what manner of spirit we are of. Our walk with Him must be constant, not on-again-off-again. Otherwise, we will seek for Him some day and not find Him."[53]

Another Look at Obedience

Earlier in the book, we talked about the important role obedience plays in the Kingdom life, and we looked at a few sample commandments. We've also discussed the fact that some of Christ's commands are weightier than others. In the next section of our book, we're going to take a closer look at some of these weightier commandments. By "weightier," I don't mean that these commandments are a heavy burden. Rather, these are some of the most *important* commandments. Happily, one of the secrets of the Kingdom Life is that when we come to love these commandments and bear fruit accordingly, we find that Christ's burden becomes even lighter.

SOME OF THE WEIGHTIER COMMANDS

28

Love: The Greatest Commandment

The only reward love seeks is someone to love. If you are looking for something else, it is not love. –Bernard of Clairvaux

When Christ is everywhere, wrath and hatred will be nowhere. –William Law

Love of our neighbor is the only door out of the dungeon of Self. –George MacDonald

Did you know that it's possible to escape this mortal life before we die? It is, although not in an absolute sense. To the extent that we learn to love as God loves—to the degree that love completely takes hold of us and becomes the dominant force in our life—to this extent we can escape this mortal life and all that is attached to it.

God is seeking true children, sons and daughters who love as He loves and who love the things He loves. Jesus tells us, " 'You shall love the Lord your God with all your heart, with all your soul, and with all your mind.' This is the first and great commandment. And the second is like it: 'You shall love your neighbor as yourself.' On these two commandments hang all the Law and the Prophets" (Matt. 22:37-40). Loving God and loving our neighbor are not only the two greatest commandments, they are *all* of God's commandments combined. When we have fulfilled the two great commandments, we have fulfilled all of God's commandments.

What does it mean to love God with our whole heart, mind, and soul? For one thing, it means that we keep His commandments. "He who has My commandments and keeps them, it is he who loves Me. And he who loves Me will be loved by My Father, and I will love him and manifest Myself to him" (John 14:21).

Is it possible to keep God's commandments without loving Him? To an extent. Obviously, if we don't love God, we're missing the greatest commandment of all. However, we can keep many of the lesser commandments—particularly the external ones—without truly loving God. The Pharisees did that. And as we've discussed, love is not the primary force behind fear obedience and dutiful obedience.

Scottish minister Henry Scougal describes our love for God this way: "Love for God is a delightful and affectionate sense of the divine perfections. It makes the soul surrender and sacrifice itself wholly unto Him. It desires above all things to please Him. It delights in nothing so much as to be in fellowship and communion with Him. Love of God means we're ready to do or suffer anything for His sake."[54]

The Victorious Cycle

Love is one of the greatest forces of the Victorious Cycle. Without true love—love of God and our neighbor—our prayers will be greatly hindered. As one author put it, "We cannot be wrong with man and right with God."[55] If we harbor hatred toward our fellow man, to a large degree all we are doing on our knees is pretending to pray. Andrew Murray observed, "A loving life is the condition of believing prayer."[56]

If we are disobedient to the two great commandments, it means very little that we obey a hundred of the lesser commands. Without love, the Kingdom Life is impossible. But what is love? To answer that question, we need only to look at Jesus and His Father.

Greatest Love Story of All Time

The eternal love between the Father and His Son is the deepest, greatest love story of all time. Their love for each other eclipses any love that has ever been felt between two humans. Christians have written tens of thousands of books, containing millions of pages, about Christ's love for *us*. Poets and composers have written thousands of hymns about this same love. Yet few books or hymns have ever been written about the deep love Christ and His Father have for each other.

Nevertheless, it was that love which sent Jesus on the most marvelous voyage that has ever been taken—or ever will be taken—in the history of the universe. That voyage brought the eternal Son of God from heaven to earth to be born as a human and to die a horrible death. To be sure, Jesus did this because He loved *us*. Yet He did so even more because He loved His Father. If it had not been His Father's will, Jesus would have never come to earth.

Jesus' entire delight, focus, and life is in His Father. He loves not only His Father, but His Father's ways, His purposes, and His commandments. He constantly thinks of His Father, and He continually talks to His Father. As Jesus told His disciples, "My food is to do the will of Him who sent Me and to finish His work" (John 4:34). Jesus is the Kingdom Life taken to perfection!

Just as His Father is the joy of Jesus' life, so Jesus longs for His Father to be the joy of our lives. After the Last Supper, Jesus tenderly prayed to His Father about us: "That they all may be one, as You, Father, are in Me, and

I in You; that they also may be one in Us, that the world may believe that You sent Me. And the glory which You gave Me I have given them, that they may be one just as We are one: I in them, and You in Me; that they may be made perfect in one" (John 17:21-23). Jesus wants us to experience the profound happiness He knows in His Father.

One of the tragedies of Christian history is that this love of Jesus for His Father was largely forgotten in Roman Catholic teaching and replaced by Jesus' supposed obsession with His earthly mother Mary. I have no doubt that Jesus loved His earthly mother in a special way, but it was not Mary that He talked about endlessly. It was always His eternal Father. In fact, when His disciples told Him that Mary and His siblings were waiting to talk to Him, Jesus "stretched out His hand toward His disciples and said, 'Here are My mother and My brothers! For whoever does the will of My Father in heaven is My brother and sister and mother' " (Matt. 12:49-50).

So Jesus made it quite clear where His heart's greatest affection lies. It is not toward Mary; it is toward His Father. Did you notice that He said His mother and brothers are those who do the "will of *My Father* in heaven"? He could just as correctly have said, "My mother and brothers are those who do *My* will." But no, he used that opportunity—just as He used so many others—to draw attention to His Father, whom He loves so dearly.

The Father's Love for Jesus

Does the Father feel the same way toward Jesus? Absolutely! His greatest joy is His Son. He delights in honoring and elevating Him. He showers His Son with gifts, powers, and distinction. As Jesus said, "All things have been delivered to Me by My Father" (Matt. 11:27). The relationship between the Father and the Son is so close that Jesus could say, "No one knows the Son except the Father" (Matt. 11:27). The Father loves His Son so much that any friend of His Son's is automatically a friend of the Father. Jesus assures us, "He who loves Me will be loved by My Father" (John 14:21).

It's hard to imagine the unspeakable anguish the Father felt watching His Son being humiliated and dying in agony. Almost all earthly fathers would rather die or suffer than have one of their children do so—particularly before their eyes. How much more so a Divine Father! I have no doubt that the darkness that followed Jesus' death was the Father's outpouring of grief at what had happened.

There are few passages of Scripture more tender than the words Jesus spoke at the moment of His arrest: "Do you think that I cannot now pray to My Father, and He will provide Me with more than twelve legions of angels?" (Matt. 26:53). I had read that passage hundreds of times, seeing nothing in it beyond the fact that Jesus was going to His death willingly. However, one day while reading it during my devotional time, the full import of what Jesus said suddenly hit me—and I found myself getting choked up.

Think about Jesus' words for a moment. The Father and Son had planned Jesus' incarnation and death before the world was even created. Yet Jesus told His apostles that if at the last moment He had found that He was not able to go through with it, His Father would have instantly intervened to save Him. I'm not saying that the Father would have abandoned us. He surely would have found another way to redeem us. But He was not going to let His beloved Son suffer *unwillingly* for even one second. Jesus only had to say the word, and twelve legions of angels—over 60,000 angels—would have instantly been at His side. That's how precious Jesus is to His Father.

Learning to Love Like God

The intense love the Father has for His Son in no way diminishes the love He feels for each of us. Love does not become diluted when it is shared among many people. Jesus says that the Father loves faithful Christians just as He loves Jesus (John 17:23).

William Law describes God's love for us in these words: "You are as much in the care of this great God and Father of all worlds and all spirits, as if He had no earthly children but you, or there was no creature for Him to love and protect but you alone. He numbers the hairs on your head. He watches over you, sleeping and waking. He has preserved you from a thousand dangers that you, nor I, know anything about."[57]

When we love our neighbors as we love ourselves, we won't harbor any mean or hurtful thoughts toward them. We would rather suffer a thousand wrongs from them than to ever wrong them ourselves. We rejoice in the blessings and righteous successes of our neighbors as if they were our own personal joys. We feel their hurts as if they were our own, and we object to any evil that befalls them. We frequently pray for their happiness, health, family, and spiritual wellbeing.

Loving our neighbor as ourselves means more than just having feeling and compassion for one particular neighbor or friend. It means we have such earnest feelings for *all* our fellow humans. William Law describes such a pervasive spirit of love as follows:

> The spirit of love does not want to be rewarded, honored, or esteemed. Its only desire is to propagate itself and become the blessing and happiness

> of everything that needs it. And therefore it meets wrath and evil and hatred and opposition with the same one will as light meets the darkness, only to overcome it with all its blessings.
>
> When love is the spirit of your life, it will have the freedom and universality of a spirit. It will always live and work in love, not because of this or that, here or there, but because the spirit of love can only love, wherever it is or goes or whatever is done to it.
>
> You may indeed do many works of love and delight in them, especially at such times as they are not inconvenient to you, or contradictory to your state or mood or occurrences in life. But the spirit of love is not in you till it is the spirit of your entire life, until you live freely, willingly, and universally according to it.[58]

Surrendering our entire lives to love does not come easily or happen overnight. For most Christians, it comes gradually with lots of setbacks. Yet, through the power of Christ, the spirit of love can control our lives.

Loving Our Brothers and Sisters

Among the other things that Jesus prayed for after the Last Supper was "that the love with which You loved Me may be in them" (John 17:26). Incredible. Jesus wants Christians to have the same marvelous love toward each other that the Father has for Him.

What would be the result if Christians had that kind of love for each other? Jesus explained, "That they all may be one, as You, Father, are in Me, and I in You; that they also may be one in Us, that the world may believe that You sent Me" (John 17:21). If we truly had God's type of love for each other, then we would be able to be one. What did Jesus say the result would be? He said the world would believe that God had sent Jesus.

Does the world believe that God sent Jesus to earth? No. And one reason they don't is that they don't see God's love among professing Christians. They see Christians bickering and arguing with each other. They have seen professing Christians imprison, murder, torture, and burn alive other Christians over doctrinal disputes. They have seen Christians slaughter one another over religious, political, and national issues.

We nonresistant Christians shouldn't pat ourselves on the back and imagine that the world doesn't see the bickering and disunity among us. I've met thousands of nonresistant Christians who are more than willing to turn the other cheek when it comes to war or personal revenge. They would gladly accept death rather than kill or hate their enemy. However, those very same Christians often find it difficult to love a brother or sister who holds different views than they on theological issues, church practices, or applications of biblical principles. Somehow they can love their enemy, but not their own brother.

Is that what Jesus had in mind when He said our love is to be perfect? "If you love those who love you, what reward have you? Do not even the tax collectors do the same? And if you greet your brethren only, what do you do more than others? Do not even the tax collectors do so? Therefore you shall be perfect, just as your Father in heaven is perfect" (Matt. 5:46-48).

Jesus said the tax collectors greeted their own brethren. Where does that put us when we refuse to do even that? Perhaps we're worse than the tax collectors. At least they loved each other! The simple truth is that it's usually much easier in practice to love our geopolitical enemy, whom we can't see, than it is to love our brother whom we can see.

John Wesley noted this about the Protestant or evangelical churches of his day: "Protestant churches too know how to persecute when they have power in their hands, even unto blood. And meanwhile, look how they also anathematize each other! They devote each other to the nethermost hell! What wrath, what contention, what malice, what bitterness, is everywhere found among them—even where they agree in essentials and only differ in the incidentals of religion!"[59]

Love is definitely one of the essential keys to the Kingdom Life. But there's another important quality we need to possess: humility.

29

True and False Humility

Lord, make me childlike. Deliver me from the urge to compete with another for place or prestige or position. –A. W. Tozer

When we reach out to live the Kingdom Life, it is so easy to develop spiritual pride. That's why humility is such an essential quality. As we become more and more obedient to New Testament commands, it's easy to exalt ourselves in our own minds. For that reason, Jesus warns us, "Whoever exalts himself will be humbled, and he who humbles himself will be exalted" (Luke 14:11). James tells us, "God opposes the proud, but gives grace to the humble" (Jas. 4:6). One of the reasons why Jesus condemned the scribes and Pharisees so strongly was their lack of humility. We cannot expect to have God's approval and favor if we're not humble.

Yet we can't cultivate humility if we don't know what it is. And that's where the problem begins. The world has little concept of true godly humility. To be sure, the world disapproves of people who are arrogant and conceited. But the world's answer to arrogance is mere skin-deep modesty. Let me give you an example.

Greg Glorious

Greg Glorious is a talented professional athlete, but he imagines he's the greatest athlete in the world. He thinks the other athletes he competes against are nowhere in his class. Although Greg is filled with enormous pride, he is also well-mannered. So in public he graciously praises those athletes he competes against. On television he frequently minimizes his own accomplishments and enlarges those of other athletes. So the world sees Greg Glorious as a very humble man.

The world cares very little about what is in Greg's heart as long as he behaves modestly and humbly in public. Greg is not a hypocrite—at least not by the world's standards. He is behaving according to the world's code of conduct. The world doesn't care if he internally takes a lot of pride in his accomplishments and feels he's better than others. In fact, most people would say that it's good that he has high self-esteem.

Godly Humility

In contrast to the world, God isn't fooled by what we say. He knows what goes on inside our hearts. To the world, the outside is paramount. To God, the inside is foremost.

So what is biblical or godly humility? It means to truly hold a modest opinion of our own importance. Godly humility has little to do with what we say, but everything to do with what we are. Humility's twin sisters are lowliness and meekness. Lowliness and meekness are not qualities the world values highly. Paul aptly describes true godly humility in his letter to the Philippians: "Let nothing be done through selfish ambition or conceit. But in lowliness of mind, let each esteem others better than himself. Let each of you look out not only for his own interests, but also for the interests of others" (Phil. 2:3-4).

Artificial Humility

Sadly, it's not just people of the world who don't understand godly humility. Many Christians don't understand it either. When we search Christian literature for a definition of humility, we typically find explanations like this one: "Spiritually, one abases himself because he realizes his sinfulness, and therefore he is willing to depend on God to meet His needs."[60]

Millions of professing Christians meet that definition of humility. However, it's merely a theological doctrine to which they give mental assent. It has little to do with true godly humility. Lots of Christians who are not humble recognize their fallen nature and see their utter need to rely on God for salvation. But true godly humility is a quality of the heart, not a theological doctrine. Let me illustrate what I mean.

The Trials of Brother Phil

Brother Phil pastors Grace Metropolitan Church in a suburban community. Although he loves serving the Lord, he has discovered that pastoring a church can bring enormous trials. When he first came to Grace Metropolitan Church, he thought he was pastoring an extremely humble congregation. That's because, to a person, the members of the congregation testified that they acknowledged their own sinfulness and unworthiness before the Lord. However, Brother Phil has since learned that holding to such doctrines has nothing to do with real humility. Let me give you a few examples.

First, there was the issue with Simon Syn. Simon will tell you that he is utterly a sinner, that no good dwells in him at all. In fact, he never tires of declaring to everyone that he is unable to do anything good. He is simply a sinner saved by grace. However, one day Brother Phil called on Simon to talk with him about a particular sin in Simon's life. Brother Phil thought this would be a nonconfrontational conversation since Simon so regularly proclaims what a sinner he is. However, to Phil's surprise, Simon was highly offended that the pastor would believe that there were any failings in his life. In fact, he was so upset that he withdrew his membership and now attends another church.

Sylvia Shrew is another member of Grace Metropoliatan Church. She often testifies at the weekly prayer meetings about how she can scarcely believe that Jesus could love such a sinner as herself. She tells others about how unworthy she is and that there is nothing in her that she could glory about. However, one day she called on Brother Phil to discuss problems in her marriage. She spewed forth a litany of complaints about her husband and his many faults. The pastor listened sympathetically and commiserated with her. He then tactfully pointed out some of Sylvia's character flaws and tried to help her see that there was fault on both sides. Sylvia responded in utter disbelief. She has character flaws? She is responsible for some of their marriage problems? Not a chance! She stormed out of the counseling session and began gossiping about Brother Phil to others in the church.

Brother Phil had appreciated that the congregation as a whole had always been receptive to his sermons against sin. That is, they were very receptive so long as he preached against sin in general, or sins common among people in the world, or minor sins of imperfection of which virtually every human is guilty.

However, one day Brother Phil decided to quit preaching about sin in general and start preaching seriously against specific sins that he realized were present in the congregation. He went through the various New Testament commandments that many, if not most, of the members were disobeying. The result? Within six months, the congregation fired Brother Phil.

What Brother Phil learned the hard way is that many Christians imagine that humility means believing in such theological doctrines as the utter depravity of man. They think humility resides in our mental processes rather than in our hearts. It's easy to say that we are sinners who can do no good. However, how we respond when someone talks to us about specific sins in our lives reveals how much humility we really have.

So let's see what we find when we move beyond hollow humility.

30

Beyond Hollow Humility

Do not let your peace depend upon the word of men. For whether they judge well or ill of you, you are not therefore any other man than who you are. –Thomas á Kempis

We must unlearn what the spirit of the world has taught us, before we can be governed by the spirit of humility. –William Law

Fifteen-century spiritual writer Thomas á Kempis describes a truly humble Christian as "one who is so contented and comforted by God, that he would just as willingly be the least among others as most other people desire to be the greatest. The humble Christian is content and at peace when he is in the lowest place as when he is in the highest one. He is just as willing to be viewed as small and of no account by others as he is to be viewed as more honorable and greater than everyone else."[61]

That probably sounds unrealistic. How could anyone honestly be as content to be viewed as of no account by others as he would to be viewed by others with great respect? The answer lies in the word *others*. The person living the Kingdom Life cares enormously what *God* thinks of him. However, he knows that what others think of him matters little.

Peggy Prodigy

Peggy Prodigy is an artist studying painting at a famous art institute. Her final grade each semester depends totally on how her professor, Dr. Deborah Dubois, judges the merits of her paintings. On various open house weekends, the institute invites the students' parents to come and view the students' paintings and sculptures. When the parents review the artwork, they nearly always talk among themselves about which works they think are outstanding and which are inferior.

Since Peggy works as an attendant at these open houses, she usually overhears such comments. Some really like her paintings, and others strongly dislike them. Do their comments affect her? Not in the least. Peggy knows that her grades depend entirely on the assessment made by Dr. Dubois. She also knows that what parents think is good art is often the very opposite of what Dr. Dubois judges to be good art. So she feels no different when she overhears them praising her paintings than when she overhears them criticizing them.

It's the same way in the Kingdom Life. Such Christians know that what other people think of them often has little in common with what God thinks of them. Francis of Assisi spoke wisely when he commented, "Blessed is the servant who esteems himself no better when he is praised and exalted by people than when he is considered worthless, simple, and despicable. For what a man is before God, that he is and nothing more."[62]

Why True Humility Is Rare

Why is true humility so hard to find? Because it goes against everything we are bombarded with from the day we are born. The world cherishes power, riches, fame, prestige, and beauty. From the time most of us were toddlers, our parents encouraged us to excel others. Schools use pride and competition to motivate students to surpass others in both academics and athletics. They hold elections for students to vote for who is the most popular. Some schools issue bumper stickers to the parents of honor students so those parents can brag about their children.

From primary school through college, we are encouraged to pursue careers that will give us prestige, wealth, and power over others. Schools and colleges also spur us to have collective pride—pride in our school, pride in our state, and pride in our country. We're supposed to think that our school is the best in the state or the nation. Why? Because *we* go there. Our country is the best country on earth. Why? Because *we* live in it. If we lived in another country, we would be told *that* country is the best on earth.

So from the time we are toddlers, we have been trained to foster pride in ourselves and in everything connected to us. No wonder humility is hard to cultivate! We've been programmed for pride, not humility. William Law aptly described this situation:

> The first state of mind we try to awaken in children is pride—which is as dangerous a passion as that of lust. We stir children up to vain thoughts of themselves, and we do everything we can to puff up their minds. We stir our youth to action by using strife and ambition. We motivate them with glory, envy, and a desire for distinction, so that they may excel others and shine in the eyes of the world. We encourage them to have honors in their eye, to scorn to be outdone by others, to accept no rival, to thirst after every instance of applause, and to be content with nothing but the highest distinctions.[63]

So it is little wonder that by the time we reach adulthood we are glutted with pride. Yet Christians imagine that because years ago they said a prayer in which they acknowledged that they were sinners and needed Christ for salvation, that means they have somehow conquered pride. In reality, all that has usually happened is that they've embraced a theological position. Their hearts are as full of pride as ever.

The Most Humble Man Who Ever Lived

There has been only one perfect example of humility here on earth, Jesus. He Himself said, "I am meek and lowly in heart" (Matt. 11:29). To have been above all creation but then lower Himself to become part of that creation is unfathomable. But it didn't stop there. He lowered Himself even more when He washed the feet of His disciples, a job normally given to the lowest of slaves. But even that pales in comparison to His allowing those very humans He had created to mock Him, hit Him, spit on Him, scourge Him, and then put Him to death as a criminal in one of the cruelest ways possible.

Although deserving of endless praise and glory, Jesus used every opportunity to draw glory away from Himself and re-direct it toward His Father. He told the unbelieving Jews, "When you lift up the Son of Man, then you will know that I am He, and that I do nothing of Myself; but as My Father taught Me, I speak these things. . . . If God were your Father, you would love Me, for I proceeded forth and came from God; nor have I come of Myself, but He sent Me" (John 8:28,42).

On another occasion He told the crowd, "I have not spoken on My own authority; but the Father who sent Me gave Me a command, what I should say and what I should speak. And I know that His command is everlasting life. Therefore, whatever I speak, just as the Father has told Me, so I speak" (John 12:49-50). Jesus behaved exactly opposite to how fallen humans behave. He went out of His way to minimize His own authority and to call attention to His Father. In contrast, our tendency is to magnify ourselves and downplay others. When we do give others credit, it's often out of a false, skin-deep modesty. Like Gregg Glorious, we publicly say modest things because that makes people admire us even more.

But there was no false modesty in Jesus. He was not jealous of his Father's authority and greatness. Rather, He was jealous *for* His Father's authority and greatness. It pained Jesus to think that He might somehow draw glory away from His Father. So He went out of His way to direct glory away from Himself. One of the most poignant examples is His encounter with the rich young ruler who asked Him about eternal life: "Now a certain ruler asked Him, saying, 'Good Teacher, what shall I do to inherit eternal life?' So Jesus said to him, 'Why do you call Me good? No one is good but One, that is, God' " (Luke 18:18-19).

Modern commentators are baffled by this incident. Why would Jesus gently rebuke this young man for calling Him good? Why would He give this man the impression that He shouldn't be called good? This makes no sense to our fallen flesh. So we dream up explanations that fit our own egos. We say things such as, "No doubt Jesus paused here, waiting for the young man to acknowledge His divinity." After all, if any of us were divine, we would surely want to call attention to the fact. If *we* were truly good, most of us would certainly let everyone know it. So we project our pride onto Jesus.

Obviously, Jesus is good in every sense of the word. So why did He say what He did? As George MacDonald explains, "He did not care to hear Himself called good. It was not of consequence to Him. He was there to let men see the goodness of the Father in whom He gloried."[64] When Jesus heard the word *good,* His thoughts immediately rose to the Father. Jesus is perfectly good, but because His goodness flows from that of the Father, He wanted His Father to receive all the glory—even if it meant directing glory away from Himself. Perfect humility!

Jesus was not only the perfectly humble Man, He was also the perfectly forgiving Man. Because one of the qualities that flows from genuine humility is forgiveness.

31

Forgiving Others

He that cannot forgive others, breaks the bridge over which he himself must pass if he would ever reach heaven; for everyone has need to be forgiven. –George Herbert

No prayers can be heard which do not come from a forgiving heart. –J. C. Ryle

If you do not forgive men their trespasses, neither will your Father forgive your trespasses. –Matt. 6:15

Wilbert Flintwinch had worked at Pembroke's Department Store for over thirty years. He began as a sales clerk and worked his way up to overseeing the men's clothing department. He had over twenty employees who worked under him, and he had the power to hire and fire these employees.

One morning Wilbert received a note that Henry Pembroke, the owner, wanted to see him. As Wilbert walked to Mr. Pembroke's office, he thought about his many experiences with the company over the years—some happy, some sad. Wilbert hoped that perhaps he was about to receive a promotion. On the other hand . . . there was the dark secret. Had Mr. Pembroke discovered it?

When Wilbert entered Mr. Pembroke's office, the store manager was there as well. After exchanging greetings and making some small talk, Mr. Pembroke invited Wilbert to sit down. "I'll get right to the point, Flintwinch," he said with a grim face. "We've discovered that you've been stealing from the company for years. And—"

"There must be some mistake!" Wilbert interrupted.

"There's no mistake," Mr. Pembroke continued. "You've been entering phony refunds on the cash register and pocketing the money."

"Why, that's absurd," Wilbert protested. "I love my job here, and I'm well paid. I have no reason to steal from the company. Show me one of these phony refunds you're talking about."

Mr. Pembroke reached across the desk and handed one of the receipts to Wilbert. After perusing it, Wilbert calmly said, "This shows the refund was given by an employee with the number 107863. That's not my employee ID number. I knew there was some mistake."

"I know it's not your ID number," Mr. Pembroke replied curtly. "It belongs to a Debbie Rawlings. However, after some checking, I've learned that no such person works here. It's a phony setup."

"Well, why accuse *me*?" Wilbert asked in feigned surprise.

"At first we didn't," Mr. Pembroke explained. "We checked the records for refunds from employee number 107863 over the years, and we found that they go back nearly ten years. During this time, nearly a million dollars in fake refunds have been given by this fictitious employee."

"I still don't see why this has anything to do with me," Wilbert contended, fighting to remain calm.

"Actually, Flintwinch, we probably would have never connected these thefts to you," Mr. Pembroke stated, "but you made one fatal slip. A refund from #107863 was issued at 8:37 a.m. last Thursday. This was before the store had even opened. So we checked the security cameras, and they show you punching keys on the cash register and taking out cash at 8:37 a.m. that day." With those words, Mr. Pembroke reached for the telephone.

"No!" Wilbert protested. "Please don't call the police! I don't want to go to jail!"

"Well, you should have thought of that before you started stealing from us."

"Please, please forgive me!" Wilbert wailed, throwing himself on Mr. Pembroke's desk. "I have absolutely no excuse. You've treated me so well through the years, and this is how I repaid you. I deserve no mercy, but think of my wife and children. I'm their sole support. I deserve to be punished, but *they* don't."

Wilbert continued crying and pleading for nearly fifteen minutes. Finally, Mr. Pembroke relented. "Okay, okay. If you return the money, I won't say anything to the police."

"But I don't have the money. I've already spent it."

"What! You've spent a million dollars. How?"

"Well," Wilbert explained, "there've been vacations, summer camp for the children, medical bills, remodeling . . ."

"Well then, I'm sorry," Mr. Pembroke interrupted, "you'll just have to sweat it out in prison."

"No!" Wilbert cried out in desperation. "Please forgive me! Please forgive me!"

This new round of pleas continued for another ten minutes or so. Finally, Mr. Pembroke relented. "All right. You don't deserve it, but I'm going to let you go free. I just don't want to see your disgusting face around here ever again. We'll mail you your final paycheck."

"Oh, thank you, thank you!" Wilbert cried out with tears of joy. "You're the most wonderful man in the world."

"You mean the biggest sucker in the world," Mr. Pembroke corrected him. "All right, get going."

"Oh, one last thing, Mr. Pembroke," Wilbert interjected. "I know I have no right to ask this, but please let me keep my job. My family depends upon this income, and with the recession on right now, I don't know how I could ever get another job. You can be sure I'll never do anything dishonest again. Not only that, but if you let me keep my job, I'll work twice as hard as ever. I can guarantee you that Pembroke's will get back it's million dollars in increased sales over the next few years."

Once again, the men talked back and forth, Wilbert pleading and Mr. Pembroke saying no. Finally, Mr. Pembroke relented. "I can't believe I'm doing this, but okay. You can keep your job. Now get out of my office before I change my mind."

Wilbert bounded down the stairs in relief. And he was true to his word. He jumped in and helped various salespeople with customers. He talked up Pembroke's Department Store with everyone he could. On the commuter train every morning and evening, he told people around him what a wonderful guy Mr. Pembroke is and what a great store he runs.

However, about two weeks after his meeting with Mr. Pembroke, Wilbert noticed something in the shirt pocket of one of his employees, Fernando Rodriguez. Wilbert didn't say anything about it, but when Fernando's shift ended, Wilbert followed him out to his car.

"Oh, Mr. Flintwinch, I didn't see you," Fernando said, startled. "What are you doing here?"

Ignoring his question, Wilbert glared at Fernando and coldly demanded, "What's that in your shirt pocket, Rodriguez?"

"My shirt pocket?" Fernando responded with a puzzled look. He reached into his pocket and pulled out a pack of sugar. "You mean this?"

"That's exactly what I mean," Wilbert fired back with a scowl. "I'm sure you know we have a zero tolerance policy here on employee theft. You took that sugar from the break room, didn't you?"

"Why, I guess so. But theft? This? I didn't even realize it was there. I usually take two packs of sugar to add to my coffee. Today, after I added the first pack, Bob came over to my table to talk, and I totally forgot to pour in the second pack."

"Do you expect me to believe that baloney?" Wilbert shot back. "This employee theft has got to stop. And the only way to kill it is with a firm, no-exceptions policy. In short, you're fired, Rodriguez!"

"But Mr. Flintwinch, why would I want to steal a pack of sugar? We've got lots of sugar at home."

"I'm sure you do," Wilbert replied coldly. "All in little white packets. How long have you been stealing sugar from the company, Rodriguez? Years and years, I can guess."

Fernando stared at Wilbert in disbelief. "But I tell you, Mr. Flintwinch, this was totally unintentional. Surely you wouldn't fire someone over a pack of sugar. Here, take it back," he said, offering the pack to Wilbert.

Wilbert jerked back his hands. "Are you trying to bribe me?" he objected. "I don't want your stolen goods. Just get out of here. I don't ever want to see you again. We'll mail you your final paycheck."

"But Mr. Flintwinch, you can't do this!" Fernando pleaded. "My family depends upon this income, and with the recession on right now, I don't know how I could get another job. Please, please!"

"You should have thought about that before you stole from the company," Wilbert replied stonily. With that, he turned his back and returned to the store.

Too Implausible!

You're no doubt thinking, "That could never happen in real life." Oh, but it does. In fact, you've probably seen Wilbert Flintwinch many times. Some of us may have seen him just this morning—when we looked in the mirror.

Undoubtedly, you recognize the story about Wilbert Flintwinch as a modern version of Jesus' parable of the unmerciful servant. Each of us becomes a Wilbert Flintwinch when we refuse to forgive our fellow man.

If this story sounds absurd, it is. It's exactly how absurdly—and how wickedly—we act when we refuse to forgive others. Whatever others have done to us is like taking a pack of sugar in comparison to what we've done to God. No one on earth would be as forgiving as Mr. Pembroke. Yet there is One who is even more forgiving.

Conditional Forgiveness

One of the things that should be explained to every new Christian—but almost never is—is that God's forgiveness is conditional. In fact, not only do preachers fail to tell new converts this essential truth, they usually proclaim the exact opposite—that God's forgiveness is unconditional. Preachers assure their listeners that if they only pray the sinner's prayer and invite Jesus into their hearts, then every past and future sin is unconditionally and permanently forgiven.

However, those living the Kingdom Life don't rely on what preachers and commentators say. They trust in what

Jesus says. In the parable of the unmerciful servant (Matt. 18:21-35), Jesus tells of a servant who owed the king an enormous sum—over a million dollars. When the servant pleaded that he could not pay what he owed and begged for mercy, the king forgave him the entire debt. Yet that same servant went out and refused to forgive the tiny amount that a fellow servant owed him.

Remember how the parable ends?

> Then his master, after he had called him, said to him, "You wicked servant! I forgave you all that debt because you begged me. Should you not also have had compassion on your fellow servant, just as I had pity on you?" And his master was angry, and delivered him to the torturers until he should pay all that was due to him. So My heavenly Father also will do to you if each of you, from his heart, does not forgive his brother his trespasses. (Matt. 18:32-35)

In this parable Jesus reveals that when God forgives us, it's conditional. The king forgave the servant all of his debt. Yet when the servant refused to forgive the debt owed to him by a fellow servant, the king rescinded his original forgiveness and reinstated the debt. Just in case we didn't get the point of the parable, Jesus drives it home in the end: "So My heavenly Father also will do to you if each of you, from his heart, does not forgive his brother his trespasses" (Matt. 18:35).

When He gave us the Lord's Prayer, Jesus only authorized us to ask for forgiveness from God to the extent that "we forgive our debtors" (Matt. 6:12). He went on to say, "For if you forgive men their trespasses, your heavenly Father will also forgive you. But if you do not forgive men their trespasses, neither will your Father forgive your trespasses" (Matt. 6:14-15).

James reinforces what Jesus teaches: "For judgment is without mercy to the one who has shown no mercy" (Jas. 2:13). So there's no point in even imagining that we're living a Kingdom Life if we are unmerciful and unforgiving. When Jesus denounced the Pharisees for "straining out a gnat and swallowing a camel," He pointed out that they had neglected "the weightier matters of the law: justice and *mercy* and faith" (Matt. 23:23-24).

So we can proclaim to the whole world how wonderful God's mercy is. We can sing how amazing His grace is. Yet all of our glorious words are drowned out by our actions when we don't forgive others. It's not that we're *like* Wilbert Flintwinch. It's that we *are* Wilbert Flintwinch.

Can anybody imagine for a moment that God would want to spend eternity in company with a Wilbert Flintwinch?

32

Judging Others

When we judge, we usurp the Lord's own office. – Francis of Sales

A criticizing spirit destroys holiness of life more easily than anything else, because it is such an eminently respectable sin. –The Kneeling Christian

You well know how to excuse and to color your own deeds, but you won't accept the excuses of others. –Thomas á Kempis

Jim Gray teaches American History at Medville High. For one of his exams each year, he requires his students to memorize the first two paragraphs of the Declaration of Independence. This year was no different. He explained to his students how the exam would work. On the assigned day, each student would be required to write down verbatim the two opening paragraphs of the Declaration. For each word they omitted or altered, they would lose two points.

Marcie Meticulous had studied very hard for this exam, and she practiced writing out those two paragraphs by memory many times until she had them down nearly perfectly. On the day of the exam, things went well, and she felt certain she had earned an A.

After the exam was over, Mr. Gray handed out the completed exams at random among the students so they could grade each other's exams. "I'm going to read aloud the first two paragraphs of the Declaration of Independence," he explained. "I want you to follow along as I read and circle every error you find on the paper you're grading. If there are words missing, mark the spot with an arrow. However, I don't want you to be too nitpicky. If the student has merely changed an article like 'the' or has made some other minor word change, you can let that pass."

Mr. Gray then read aloud the two introductory paragraphs, and the students graded the exam papers they had been given. When he was finished reading, Mr. Gray told the students, "Now add up the errors you've noted, subtract two points for each one, and write the student's score at the top of the page. I also want you to put 'graded by' and then write your name. Then hand the graded exam back to the student to whom it belongs."

Mr. Gray gave the students time to look over their papers. When the bell rang, he announced, "Leave your exam on my desk on your way out. If you've discovered an error in the grading or if you feel the grader was too finicky, stop by during my free period and we can talk about it."

Marcie had been disappointed to discover she had received an 86 on the exam. But her ears pricked up when she heard Mr. Gray's announcement. Kenny Childress had graded her paper, and she felt certain that he had graded her much too stringently. So during Mr. Gray's free period, she stopped by his classroom.

"Hello, Mr. Gray," she greeted him.

"Oh, hi Marcie. What can I do for you?"

"Well, at the end of class you said that if we felt our grader had been overly picky, we should see you. Kenny Childress graded my paper, and I think he was way too finicky."

"Okay. Let's have a look at it," Mr. Gray replied cheerfully. He then found Marcie's exam among the papers on his desk.

Marcie pointed out two places where she had substituted "that" for "which." Also, she had written "those ends," instead of "these ends." She had also used "the Creator" instead of "their Creator" and "inalienable" instead of "unalienable."

"Yes, I see your point, Marcie," Mr. Gray reassured her. "Those are fairly minor errors. Kenny is certainly an exacting grader."

"Oh, thank you, Mr. Gray," Marcie exclaimed with a sigh of relief. "Those minor errors cost me ten points. So that means I get a 96, right?"

"Perhaps," Mr. Gray replied. "But first I need to check something. Whose paper did *you* grade?"

Puzzled, Marcie responded, "Janet Holt's."

Mr. Gray flipped through the stack of exam papers and pulled out Janet Holt's. He then studied her corrected paper for a moment.

"Hmm. How strange," he commented. "You feel it was too picky for Kenny to deduct two points for 'inalienable' instead of 'unalienable,' but you did the exact same thing on Janet's paper. You also marked her paper wrong for substituting 'that' for 'which.' And you deducted two points for 'those forms' instead of 'the forms.' I'm sorry, Marcie, but I'm afraid I can't change your score. You were just as exacting in your grading as Kenny. You can hardly ask to be graded more leniently than you graded Janet's paper."

"But, Mr. Gray," Marcie pleaded, "that's not fair. You didn't tell us in advance that you would grade us the same way we graded others. If I had known, I would have been lenient with Janet."

"I think it's very fair," Mr. Gray responded. "Now, if you'll excuse me, I've got some other work I have to do."

What About in Real Life?

What do you think? Was Mr. Gray being fair? Should he have let the students know in advance that they would be graded the same way they graded others? Would Marcie have graded Janet's paper differently if she had known it would affect her own grade?

I ask those questions because the same principle applies in the Real world of eternity. Jesus lets us decide how leniently or harshly we want to be graded on Judgment Day. But unlike Mr. Gray, He *has* told us in advance that we will be graded the same way we grade others. Jesus warns us, "Judge not, that you be not judged. For with what judgment you judge, you will be judged; and with the measure you use, it will be measured back to you" (Matt. 7:1-2).

That's about as straightforward as a person can put something. We get to choose how we're going to be judged in eternity. We can choose to be judged harshly, or we can choose to be judged leniently. We have the same choice Marcie had, except this time it doesn't determine some temporal grade on a report card. It determines our eternal destiny!

Deciding Who Is and Who Is Not a Christian

Alexander Campbell, one of the leaders of the nineteenth-century Restoration Movement, lamented, "This plan of making our own nest and fluttering over our own brood; of building our own tent, and confining all goodness and grace to our noble selves and the 'elect few' who are like us—this is the quintessence of sublimated pharisaism. The Pharisees of old were but babes in comparison to the modern."[65] Ironically, despite his warning, many of Campbell's followers did the very thing their founder condemned.

I find it incredible how so many ordinary Christians are quick to make pronouncements on where other professing Christians stand with God in eternity. It's common to hear Christians speak about other individuals or entire churches and glibly say, "Oh, they're not Christians," or "He's not a Christian." If they're speaking about a Hindu, Buddhist, or someone who doesn't claim to be a Christian, that's appropriate.

However, many Christians are quick to make such pronouncements about other professing Christians. On what basis do they condemn their brother or sister to hell? Typically it's because of the other person's theology. How many people did Jesus condemn to hell because of their theology? As far as I know, no one. Yet in today's spiritual world of easy believism, untold millions of Christians believe that God's grace covers every kind of sordid sin imaginable—except a theological error.

Now, please don't get me wrong. Jesus said, "Many are called, but few are chosen," and "Narrow is the gate and difficult is the way which leads to life, and there are few who find it" (Matt. 22:14; 7:14). I'm not so spiritually naïve as to think that everyone who professes to be a Christian will inherit eternal life. In fact, I'm very concerned about where many millions of professing Christians actually stand with God. That's the primary reason I write the books I do.

It is one thing to be concerned about the spiritual standing of others. It is an entirely different thing to make dogmatic pronouncements. If we condemn others to eternal punishment because of what we think are their theological errors, then we had better hope our theology is perfect. Otherwise, we've just denied ourselves eternal life.

The Speck in Your Brother's Eye

Jesus asks each of us the question, "Why do you look at the speck in your brother's eye, but do not consider the plank in your own eye? Or how can you say to your brother, 'Let me remove the speck from your eye'; and look, a plank is in your own eye? Hypocrite! First remove the plank from your own eye, and then you will see clearly to remove the speck from your brother's eye" (Matt. 7:3-5).

I've heard numerous sermons and read quite a few books and periodicals about this passage in which the speaker or author somehow fancies that Jesus actually *wants* us to look for the speck in our brother's eye. The argument usually goes something like this: Jesus didn't say that we are not supposed to look for the speck in our brother's eye. He only told us to first remove the plank from our own eye, so we could see clearly to remove the speck from our brother's eye. Yet I can't help but wonder if that's like saying, "Jesus didn't tell the mob they couldn't stone the adulterous woman. He only said that the one without sin was to throw the first stone"?

What do the commentators say it means to remove the plank from our own eye? Some say, "This means that you too have to acknowledge that you are a sinner before approaching your brother about the speck in his eye." Others say, "Getting the plank out of your own eye means that you need to approach your brother in love and humility." Still others say, "The plank means that self needs to get out of the picture. When you speak to your brother about the speck in his eye, you have to be thinking only of *his* welfare. You should not receive any satisfaction in pointing out the speck in his eye." Perhaps these commentators are correct.

However, personally I think we're missing the point. I think Jesus is saying He doesn't want us *ever* to be looking at the speck or mote in our brother's eye. That's because we will *always* have a plank or beam in our own eye. The plank is our own sins. Why are our sins a plank or beam in comparison to the speck in our brother's eye? Because we know far more about our own sins than we do about anyone else's.

Consider for a moment: How would you feel if you just learned that everything that's been said in your home or car over the past two months has been recorded? What if someone told you that the recording is going to be played back to your congregation next Sunday? Your whole church is going to hear every argument with your spouse. Every angry or impatient word spoken. Every unkind thing said about someone else. Every complaint. Every bit of gossip passed on. Would any of us be comfortable with that?

Let's go further. How would we like everything inside our minds and hearts to be publicly revealed? Every instance of pride and vanity. Every jealous or envious thought. Everything selfish, unclean, ungodly, resentful, judgmental, hurtful, unloving, hateful, dark, petty, worldly, boastful, or unkind. Added all together, they make quite a large plank or beam, don't they? When we get rid of that plank—when we are entirely without sin—then we can look at the speck in our brother's eye. Actually, when we reach that point, we'll be so full of love and humility we won't even be thinking about other people's faults.

Can We Confront Sin?

Does this mean we can't talk to others about sin in their lives, or that we can't try to correct what we believe are theological errors? No, Jesus' words don't mean any of those things. As with every other Bible teaching, we have to look at the *totality* of what the Scriptures say on the subject of judging others. We should take Matthew 7 very seriously. At the same time, we have to take Matthew 18 very seriously: "If your brother sins against you, go and tell him his fault between you and him alone. If he hears you, you have gained your brother. But if he will not hear, take with you one or two more, that 'by the mouth of two or three witnesses every word may be established.' And if he refuses to hear them, tell it to the church. But if he refuses even to hear the church, let him be to you like a heathen and a tax collector" (Matt. 18:15-17).

Does Matthew 18 nullify Matthew 7? Not at all, for they are talking about two entirely different kinds of sin. In Matthew 7, Jesus tells us not to be looking at the speck or mote in our brother's eye. A speck is tiny. The specks in our brother's eye are imperfections and minor sins that we should overlook in love. The sins spoken of in Matthew 18 are serious sins. They are so serious that our brother will be excommunicated or put out of the church because of them. We *must* talk to our brother about these kinds of sin, for his eternal life is at stake.

So Jesus commands us not to look for specks in our brother's eye. At the same time, Jesus commands us to talk to our brother when he is in serious sin. Love requires both these things. With that in mind, let me tell you a story about a Christian woman who learned a valuable lesson about judging others. I haven't introduced her yet. Her name is Paula Pious.

33

Paula Pious Meets Tara and Jim

Judge nothing rashly concerning the words or deeds of others. –Thomas á Kempis

The constant need for a Christian to go counter to popular trends may easily develop into a sour habit of faultfinding and turn him into a critic of other men's lifestyles, without charity. –George Verwer

In chapter 22, we talked about the New Testament teachings on modest dress and adornment. When Paula Pious first decided to live by these teachings, her obedience was solely Type 2 dutiful servant obedience. She obeyed God because He gave these commands, and she wanted to please God. Inwardly, however, she wished He had never given such rules. She hated the way she looked without makeup, and she sorely missed her glittering jewelry and designer clothes.

However, she could now look down on other women who were disobedient in these areas. And that gave her great pleasure. In fact, she thought she could decipher everything about other people's relationships with Christ merely by looking at how they groomed and dressed themselves.

Ugh! she thought one day when she walked past a woman in the supermarket aisle wearing heavy makeup, artificially bright magenta hair, tight jeans, and a Jesus T-shirt. *What worldliness! I wonder what kind of Christian she thinks she is?*

Paula was only picking up a few groceries that day, so she decided to carry her sacks out to her car rather than use a cart. Glancing at her watch as she walked out of the store, she stepped off the curb awkwardly, twisted her ankle, and tumbled to the ground. Cans and oranges rolled across the parking lot.

"Oh, no! Are you hurt?" a kind voice asked her.

Feeling her ankle, Paula slowly responded, "I'm not sure. My ankle really hurts."

"Well, just sit here on the sidewalk and don't move," the voice replied. "My husband will be here in just a minute, and I'll have him check it. He's a paramedic."

Paula turned to see who her benefactor was. She gulped as she saw the woman with the bright magenta hair.

"By the way, I'm Tara," the woman said cheerfully as she picked up Paula's groceries.

"I'm glad to meet you," Paula forced herself to say. "I'm Paula." She struggled not to roll her eyes when Tara's husband joined them. He had long hair and a ring in one ear and was wearing a Jesus T-shirt that matched his wife's.

"Hi, I'm Jim," he introduced himself cheerfully. Tara explained what had happened, and her husband checked Paula's ankle.

"I don't think anything's broken," he reassured her. "But we can take you to the emergency room if you like."

"No, that's not necessary," Paula replied. "I think I'll be okay if I go home and give it some rest."

"Do you live close by?" Tara asked.

"No . . . I mean, yes. I live about a mile from here. I'd phone my husband Jeff to come get me, but he's out of town."

"No problem," Jim announced, his long hair blowing in the breeze. "We'll help you to the passenger seat of your car, and then Tara can drive your car to your house. I'll follow in our car."

Paula meekly assented, then thought, *Oh, no! I don't want these creeps to know where I live. They'll probably rob me. Why did Jeff have to be gone this week?*

Jim and Tara helped Paula to her car and drove her home. They then helped her to bed.

"We need to put an ice pack on your ankle," Jim explained. "Do you have one?"

"Actually, I don't."

"Do you have an Ace bandage?"

"I'm afraid not," Paula replied, shaking her head.

"Don't worry," Jim reassured her. "We've got an ice pack in our freezer. We don't live very far away, so I'll run over and get it. I'll be going right by Walgreens, so I'll pick up an Ace bandage. Tara will stay with you. Meanwhile, let's get your ankle elevated."

Using some pillows, Jim elevated Paula's ankle. "Oh, I almost forgot," Jim added. "Do you have any Advil or aspirin?"

"Yes, there's some Advil in the bathroom," Paula replied.

"Great. Tara can get it for you while I'm at Walgreens," Jim declared as he headed for the front door.

Paula and Tara had a pleasant chat while Jim was gone. He was back in twenty minutes, triumphantly displaying an ice pack, an Ace bandage, and even a pair of crutches.

"I had forgotten we still had these crutches lying around our basement. A few years ago Tara sprained her ankle while ice skating. I think you'll find them useful."

Jim carefully wrapped Paula's ankle with the Ace bandage and placed the ice pack on it. "You should keep the ice pack on for twenty or thirty minutes several times a day," Jim explained.

"Thank you *so* much," Paula responded with a lump in her throat. She then reached for her purse. "How much do I owe you for the bandage?"

"Not a thing!" Jim replied firmly.

Jim and Tara made sure Paula was comfortable and that she had everything she needed. "Paula, you get some rest now," Tara advised. "I'll be back around six with supper." Tara waved off Paula's protests as she and Jim headed for the door.

Tara was not only back at six, but she checked on Paula every day that week. She brought more meals, and even cleaned Paula's house.

What Paula Learned

As Paula got to know Tara and looked past her appearance, she realized what a sincere Christian Tara was and what deep love she had for others. In fact, she had to admit that Tara surpassed her when it came to the second great commandment.

This brought Paula to some real soul searching. She realized that she couldn't assess everyone's relationship with God based solely on dress and adornment. She could perhaps accurately assess their level of obedience in the area of modesty, but not their whole relationship with God.

As she examined herself, Paula recognized something else. Something dark she didn't want to admit. But she finally faced up to it. She realized she actually resented people who dressed more stylishly than she and who adorned themselves more. But why? Paula asked herself,

Do I resent Christians who use tobacco? No. In fact, she was happy that being a Christian had protected her from tobacco and all of the health problems that go with it—not to speak of the added expense. She didn't envy those who "get to smoke." She delighted in being free from tobacco.

She finally realized her problem: She didn't delight in God's laws on modesty and adornment. She obeyed those laws, but she didn't delight in them. That's why she resented others who didn't follow them. Paula also realized that if the only way she could obey God's commandments on dress and adornment was to feel superior to those who dressed immodestly, then there was little to gain by obeying God. Self-righteousness, spiritual pride, and resentment are greater sins than immodesty.

Paula's obedience in this area has now grown from dutiful obedience to love obedience. She appreciates that God's laws on modesty are for her own good. She is glad to follow His counsel. This new appreciation of God's laws on modesty and adornment has helped her not to be resentful or feel self-righteous toward those who dress immodestly. They're the ones missing out on the blessings that flow from obedience. She also appreciates that their disobedience may not be a matter of the heart at all. They may think they are dressing modestly. Perhaps they never received any teaching in this area. Or they could be following their preacher's counsel.

Paula in no way minimizes the sin of immodesty. On the other hand, she no longer elevates God's laws on modesty above God's laws on love. She delights in dressing and adorning herself modestly. But she delights even more in growing to love her neighbors. Paula is discovering the joys of the Kingdom Life.

What Tara Later Learned

One day when Tara was visiting Paula, she asked, "Listen, I hope you don't think I'm being too nosey, Paula, but can I ask you a question?"

"If it's too personal I may not answer it," Paula replied with a chuckle, "but go ahead and ask."

"Well, ever since I met you I've wanted to ask you why you dress so weird."

Paula couldn't keep from laughing out loud. "Why do *I* dress weird? That's a good one. Here all along I've been wanting to ask you why *you* dress so weird."

Both ladies howled with laughter. When they finally recovered, Paula invited Tara to sit down at the table with her so she could show her something in the Bible. She opened her Bible to 1 Timothy 2 and asked Tara to read verses eight through ten: "I desire therefore that the men pray everywhere, lifting up holy hands, without wrath and doubting; in like manner also, that the women adorn themselves in modest apparel, with propriety and moderation, not with braided hair or gold or pearls or costly clothing, but, which is proper for women professing godliness, with good works."

"So I dress the way I do out of modesty and simplicity," Paula explained. "The irony is that throughout most of Christian history, from the time of Jesus until about 1900, a Christian woman could dress modestly and simply without looking strange to others. It's only in the last century that modest Christian women have stood out as different."

"Well, sure," Tara replied as she chewed on her gum, "but I always thought the way I dress was modest. I don't show much skin."

"Listen, I'm not here to judge you," Paula reassured her, "and it's true that you cover most of your skin. However, what you don't realize is that your jeans and T-shirt reveal every curve of your body. I can assure you that it attracts men's attention."

"I . . . I never thought of that," Tara responded soberly. "Hmm. You've made me think. It honestly never occurred to me that my getup was immodest. Now, mind you, I'm not going to dress like you, but I *am* going to talk with Jim about this tonight."

Sins That Easily Ensnare Us

Judging is truly a sin that can easily ensnare anyone, especially those who set their sights on the Kingdom Life. As we've said, it's also a very serious sin. Next we're going to look at another sin that easily ensnares us. The problem with this next sin is that most Christians think it's a minor offense. But it's not.

34

Gossip: The Pervasive Sin

Speak evil of no man. –Titus 3:2

It is evil to publicize the faults and infirmities of others. –Samuel Logan Brengle

Let no gossiper say that he meant no harm. Our Lord, who knows the hearts of men, has said, "Out of the abundance of the heart the mouth speaks." –Francis of Sales

Very few, if any, Christians are free from gossip. It is one of the most pervasive sins in our churches. Even Christians who live the Kingdom Life in most other areas often succumb to this evil. As James said, "The tongue is a little member and boasts great things. See how great a forest a little fire kindles! And the tongue is a fire, a world of iniquity" (Jas. 3:5-6).

What Is Gossip?

My dictionary defines gossip as "idle talk or rumor, especially about the personal or private affairs of others."[66] Some Christians have the mistaken notion that idle talk about others is not gossip as long as it is true. However, that isn't so.

The word gossip comes from an Old English noun *godsibb*, a combination of *God* + *sibb*, meaning a godparent. Since godparents were usually close friends of the family or relatives, they knew a lot about the personal matters of their godchildren's lives. Sadly, godparents often passed on juicy personal information about their godchildren to others. So *godsibb* eventually came to mean not only a godparent but also idle talk about someone else's personal affairs. Just because something is absolutely true does not change the fact that it's gossip. When we talk about the failings, faults, embarrassments, and private affairs of others, we are gossiping.

Does that mean it's always wrong to talk about other people? No, normally it's perfectly fine to relate good news and encouraging comments about others. It's fine to announce that Susan has recovered from an illness or that Joe gave an outstanding series of lessons at a recent Bible school.

However, for some dark reason, Christians find it far more interesting to talk about the failings and faults of their fellow Christians than about their victories and accomplishments in Christ. Bad news usually travels a lot faster than good news. Somehow, many Christians feel that uplifting news doesn't make for very interesting conversation.

Because most of us know in our hearts that talking about the faults and failings of others is wrong, we've come up with ingenious ways to dress up our gossip in godly clothing.

Saintly Sue

Saintly Sue would certainly never gossip about anyone. She sees herself as an "intercessory prayer warrior." On her way back from Wal-Mart one Wednesday morning, Sue stopped by the house of her Christian friend, Rita. After some small talk, Sue informed Rita in a concerned voice, "We need to pray for Conrad and Alice Martin."

"Oh, why's that?" Rita replied, her ears pricking up.

"Well, they're having a lot of marital problems right now," she explained in a hushed tone. Shaking her head, she continued, "They're constantly arguing. In fact, I hear they don't even eat at the same table. I'm really concerned that they may end up separating."

"Really?" Rita replied in pious amazement. "How long has this been going on? You'd never know it to look at them in church."

"Well, from what I hear . . ."

It all sounds so pious. It's so easy for Sue and Rita to pretend they're not gossiping about the Martins. If Saintly Sue honestly examined her heart, she would know that she didn't really talk to Rita about the Martins' marriage because she has godly concern for them. In fact, she rarely intercedes for them in private. The plain truth is that she likes to gossip, but she has enough savvy to dress up her gossip in spiritual clothing.

Why Gossip Is So Serious

"Well, what's so bad about a little gossip?" some may be thinking. "Isn't it a rather minor shortcoming, like a petty traffic infraction?" No, indeed. It is a violation of the second greatest commandment: "You shall love your neighbor as yourself" (Matt. 22:39).

William Law put it this way: "You know how it hurts you to be made the jest and ridicule of other people. You know how it grieves you to be robbed of your reputation and deprived of the favorable opinion of your neighbors. If, therefore, you expose others to scorn and contempt in any degree, or if it pleases you to see or hear of their frailties and infirmities, you are very far from loving such people as yourself. In fact, you may be justly supposed to have as much hatred for them as you have love for yourself."[67]

Jesus warns us, "Whoever says to his brother, 'Raca!' shall be in danger of the council. But whoever says, 'You fool!' shall be in danger of hell fire" (Matt. 5:22). No, the gossiper doesn't have the courage to say to his brother's face, "Raca," a word of contempt. Nor is he daring enough to say, "You fool," to his face. Instead, he does far worse. He damages his brother's reputation in the eyes of others so that they will hold his brother in contempt. He makes everyone view his brother as a fool. Yet, like the coward he is, the gossiper does it behind his brother's back. Not only that, like a Judas, he pretends to be his brother's friend.

When we gossip about our brother, not only do we wrong him, but we also wrong Jesus. In Matthew 25, Jesus said that when we feed a hungry brother or visit him in prison, we are doing it to Christ. By the same token, then, when we inflict injury on our brother through gossip, we inflict it on Christ. Remember, Jesus died for the brother we're holding up to ridicule.

No wonder the Scriptures repeatedly condemn gossip. "You shall not go about as a talebearer among your people; nor shall you take a stand against the life of your neighbor: I am the Lord" (Lev. 19:16). James tells us, "If anyone among you thinks he is religious, and does not bridle his tongue but deceives his own heart, this one's religion is useless" (Jas. 1:26).

Gossip is included in what the New Testament calls "evil speaking." Paul wrote, "Let all bitterness, wrath, anger, clamor, and evil speaking be put away from you, with all malice. And be kind to one another, tenderhearted, forgiving one another, just as God in Christ forgave you" (Eph. 4:31-32). So Paul contrasts evil speaking with being kind to one another and tenderhearted. Gossip is neither kind nor tenderhearted.

Peter contrasts evil speaking with Christian love. He writes, "Since you have purified your souls in obeying the truth through the Spirit in sincere love of the brethren, love one another fervently with a pure heart . . . laying aside all malice, all deceit, hypocrisy, envy, and all evil speaking, as newborn babes, desire the pure milk of the word, that you may grow thereby" (1 Pet. 1:22; 2:1-2).

When Gossip Becomes Slander

Up to this point, we've been talking about gossip that is true, and we have seen how serious a sin it is. However, gossip is rarely totally true. Often the gossiper does not have firsthand information. Rather, he is passing on rumors or tales that were slowly altered as they were handed by one person to another. At other times, the gossiper may be relating truthful matters of which he has personal knowledge. Yet he may omit certain facts that would put the other person in a better light. Or there may be extenuating matters of which the gossiper has no knowledge.

In short, in most instances gossipers are not only guilty of idle, hurtful talk, but also of slander. This is because they pass on false and defamatory information about others. Slander puts us even more at enmity with God. "Whoever secretly slanders his neighbor, him I will destroy" (Ps. 101:5). And again: "You give your mouth to evil, and your tongue frames deceit. You sit and speak against your brother; you slander your own mother's son" (Ps. 50:19-20).

William Law gave this poignant description of a particular gossiper: "She is hardened and cruel in evil-speaking for the same reason that cutthroats are inhuman and cruel—because she has been so long used to murder the reputation of her neighbors. She has killed all her own family over and over."[68]

Why Do Christians Gossip?

In light of the seriousness of gossip, why do most Christians engage in it? One reason is that, in most circles, gossip makes for entertaining conversation, and people want to have something interesting to talk about. They don't want to be perceived as dull and uninteresting. And so they turn to gossip. This, of course, is a terrible indictment of both the gossiper and those who listen to him. Why do so many of us find it titillating to talk about the sins, imperfections, problems, and private affairs of others? Does it not reveal something very dark deep inside us?

Jesus said, "Out of the abundance of the heart the mouth speaks. A good man out of the good treasure of his heart brings forth good things, and an evil man out of the evil treasure brings forth evil things. I say to you that for every idle word men may speak, they will give account of it in the day of judgment. For by your words you will be justified, and by your words you will be condemned" (Matt. 12:34-37). So the ultimate cause of gossip is something wrong inside a person's heart. And if he doesn't change, the consequences will be serious indeed.

What other things does gossip reveal about a person's heart? Many people gossip because they think they enhance themselves by painting others in a bad light. The world would say such gossipers have "low self-esteem." However, the real problem is that they lack godly humility. A truly humble person has no desire to artificially enhance his image in the eyes of others. His focus is on his standing before God. He knows that tearing down the reputation of others will not raise his standing before God. Rather, it will have the opposite effect. Building up his brothers and sisters—not tearing them down—will raise his value in God's eyes.

Another cause of gossip is envy. Perhaps another person is more attractive, earns more money, holds a more prominent position in the church, or has a more successful ministry than the gossiper. The gossiper cannot take these things away from that other person. But the gossiper can take something else away from that person—his reputation. William Law writes, "When you despise and ridicule a man, it is with no other end but to make him ridiculous and contemptible in the eyes of other men, and in order to prevent their esteem of him."[69]

George Verwer, the founder of the missionary organization Operation Mobilization, writes, "Envy is particularly prevalent in Christian circles. It is so easy to be jealous of another's talents. A Christian psychiatrist in India wrote to tell me that he believed that 80 percent of people's problems stem from bitterness and envy in their hearts. Until we are willing—and it is a question of the will—to let Christ's blood, love, and forgiveness wash them out of our hearts, we shall be crippled by them."[70]

The Cure for Gossip

Happily, gossip can be cured. Since gossip is ultimately a problem of the heart, the starting place is a thorough, honest examination of our hearts. Each person should ask himself, "What causes me to gossip?" If we're not sure, we should pray that God will help us to determine the real cause. Then we should pray for His Spirit to cleanse us of whatever defects in our hearts lead us to gossip. However, we shouldn't imagine that God will do all the work for us. He wants us to participate in the process of conquering this sin. The practical steps we will need to take will vary based on the cause of our gossiping.

Perhaps we gossip out of a desire to be interesting conversationalists. If so, we need to find other topics to talk about. If we find that other topics don't readily come to mind when we're in conversations, then we should plan our conversations ahead of time. We should take stock of some uplifting—or at least neutral—subjects to talk about. What good news do we know about various brothers and sisters? What can we say about friends, family members, or others in our spiritual circles that will build up those people? If we think about such topics and events beforehand, they will come to our minds more readily in the middle of a conversation.

If we still find it hard to have uplifting things to talk about, it may help if we read more. Reading good spiritual literature should give us a storehouse of worthwhile inspiring things to converse about. However, our reading doesn't have to be limited to spiritual works. If we regularly read informative literature, this too will help supply us with meaningful subjects to talk about.

In the end, we may have to simply accept the fact that we won't be as entertaining as we once were. But to be an interesting conversationalist at the expense of others is simply not acceptable for someone living the Kingdom Life.

Paul's exhortation on the things we should meditate about is also an appropriate measure of what things we should talk about: "Finally, brethren, whatever things are true, whatever things are noble, whatever things are just, whatever things are pure, whatever things are lovely, whatever things are of good report, if there is any virtue and if there is anything praiseworthy—meditate on these things" (Phil. 4:8).

Overcoming Jealousy

What if we determine that jealousy is behind much of our gossiping? One of the surest ways to defeat jealousy is to pray for the very people we're jealous of. And we shouldn't just pray for them in a general way. We should pray that God will bless them in those specific areas of which we're envious. Do we envy someone's successful ministry? We should pray that God will make his ministry even more fruitful. Do we envy someone who has more friends than we do? We should pray that God will give her even more friends. Yes, it will be like driving nails through our flesh to pray in this manner. However, if we persevere, God will help us to root out all jealousy from our hearts.

Gossip Partners

If you're serious about conquering the sin of gossip, analyze to whom you mainly gossip. You may discover that it is mainly one or two people. Too often what people call "close friendships" are really gossip partnerships. Although both genders can develop gossip partnerships, it happens more often among women. Many women forge close bonds with other women based upon gossip relationships. They gossip about their husbands, their children, their parents, their neighbors, members of their congregation, and even other friends.

Whether you are male or female, if you find yourself in such a partnership, you need to have a serious talk with your gossip partner. Explain that you realize that the two of you regularly gossip about others. Further, tell your friend that you've made a commitment to God to stop gossiping. You can then ask your friend to stop you if you ever start gossiping about someone. Explain that you will do the same if he or she starts to gossip. Encourage the other person to make a similar commitment to God.

If your relationship is a true friendship, you will be able to end your gossiping and still have plenty of other things to talk about. If you find there isn't a whole lot to talk about once the gossip stops, the relationship probably needed to end anyway.

Paul had a remedy for idle talk. Speaking about younger widows, he said, "They learn to be idle, wandering about from house to house, and not only idle but also gossips and busybodies, saying things which they ought not. Therefore I desire that the younger widows marry, bear children, manage the house, give no opportunity to the adversary to speak reproachfully" (1 Tim. 5:13-14).

In other words, gossiping is often the byproduct of having too much idle time. If that is your situation, then find useful work to fill that time. If you are actively pursuing the Kingdom Life, you will view free time as an opportunity both to enrich your prayer life and to serve Christ in kingdom work. As an old proverb expresses it, "Idle hands are the devil's work tools."

Can Someone's Sin Never Be Spoken Of?

Am I saying that all sin should be kept hidden from other Christians? Not necessarily. Sometimes it's right and necessary to reveal someone's sin as part of church discipline and for the protection of the congregation. But this should be handled by the steps set forth in Matthew 18, not through gossip.

An example of such a situation occurred in a certain church. A man who attended the church was accused of molesting a boy in the congregation. The pastor privately but thoroughly investigated all of the facts. He heard the victim's account of the incident, and he confronted the accused with that information. The accused admitted to wrongdoing. The police were notified in accordance with the law.

The next Sunday, after the service was over, the pastor called all of the heads of households into a private meeting in the church library. He related the facts they needed to know about the situation. He did not go into explicit details, as they did not need to know them. He told the family heads enough to be on guard concerning the wrongdoer and to safeguard their families. There was no need for his hearers to discuss the matter further. Nor was there any reason to spread the news to others who had no reason to know about it.

The Listener's Guilt

Up until now we've been talking about gossipers. But it's rather hard to gossip without a listener. The one who listens to gossip bears nearly as much guilt as the speaker. So what should we do if someone starts gossiping in our presence?

No one living the Kingdom Life should let himself become a party to gossip by being a willing listener. When we find ourselves in a conversation that turns into gossip, we should first try to gently redirect the conversation to another subject. If the gossip persists, we may want to simply walk away from the discussion. If the gossiper is a friend or someone with whom we have a sufficient spiritual relationship, we might tactfully say something like, "Uh-oh. I think we've crossed the line now into gossip. Let's talk about something else." Of course, we shouldn't do this with a self-righteous spirit.

The most effective way to extinguish gossip completely is to go to the person who is the subject of gossip and tell him what is being said. We don't have to tell him who is spreading the gossip, but we can say, "There's a rumor circulating that you . . ." This gives him the opportunity to give his side of the story. If it turns out that the gossip about him is clearly false, we can then go back to the ones who are spreading the gossip and tell them what we've learned. We can urge them to contact the people to whom they've spread the false story and get the matter corrected.

A Hard Habit to Break

If you've been a gossiper most of your life, you will find that it won't be easy to break the habit. Don't give up or get discouraged if you find yourself slipping back into old habits. Just pray that much more intensely for victory. Press ahead with the assurance that such victory will come with time. Make sure that gossip is a daily subject of your prayers. Examine yourself before God at the end of each day. Have you gossiped about anybody? If so, confess it before God and ask His forgiveness. And pray for more power to defeat this evil habit.

What's Next?

This brings us to the final section of this book, where we'll be talking about money, possessions, and the Kingdom Life. Just like gossip is a hard habit to break, so are wrong habits on the use of money and possessions.

35

What About Our Possessions?

Most evangelicals have swallowed wholesale the competitive accumulation of possessions. –George Verwer

Do not look at the lives of other Christians to learn how to spend your money. Rather look to the Scriptures. –William Law

One day a young man approached Jesus with a question. In itself, that was nothing unusual. Lots of people approached Jesus with questions. However, the answer Jesus gave to this particular young man has bothered Christians enormously for centuries. Let's read the account together.

> Now behold, one came and said to Him, "Good Teacher, what good thing shall I do that I may have eternal life?" So He said to him, "Why do you call Me good? No one is good but One, that is, God. But if you want to enter into life, keep the commandments." He said to Him, "Which ones?" Jesus said, "'You shall not murder,' 'You shall not commit adultery,' 'You shall not steal,' 'You shall not bear false witness,' 'Honor your father and your mother,' and, 'You shall love your neighbor as yourself.' " The young man said to Him, "All these things I have kept from my youth. What do I still lack?"
>
> Jesus said to him, "If you want to be perfect, go, sell what you have and give to the poor, and you will have treasure in heaven; and come, follow Me." But when the young man heard that saying, he went away sorrowful, for he had great possessions. Then Jesus said to His disciples, "Assuredly, I say to you that it is

> hard for a rich man to enter the kingdom of heaven. And again I say to you, it is easier for a camel to go through the eye of a needle than for a rich man to enter the kingdom of God." (Matt. 19:16-24)

Jesus' answer makes everyone squirm: "If you want to be perfect, go, sell what you have and give to the poor, and you will have treasure in heaven; and come, follow Me." Let's analyze this statement. It actually contains three separate directives: 1) "go, sell what you have," 2) "give to the poor," and 3) "come, follow Me."

Let's first focus on "go, sell what you have." Here Jesus bids this young man to dispossess his soul from material things. We shouldn't imagine that Jesus is singling out this particular rich man, for Jesus says something very similar to all of us: "If anyone comes to Me and does not hate his father and mother, wife and children, brothers and sisters, yes, and his own life also, he cannot be My disciple. And whoever does not bear his cross and come after Me cannot be My disciple. . . . Likewise, whoever of you does not forsake all that he has cannot be My disciple" (Luke 14:26-27,33).

Dispossessing Our Souls of Things

Nineteenth-century Scottish pastor and author George MacDonald made some penetrating observations about this young man, which I've condensed below:

◈◈◈◈◈◈◈◈◈

This young man was probably thinking, "There's nothing like this in the Law! Why should I have to give up all I have?" But in return for eternal life, was it really that hard to let dead things drop? To turn his back on mammon and follow Jesus? Yes, for him, it was. And most of us are no different.

Jesus wanted to set this young man free and make him a child of the kingdom, an heir of eternal life. For he was a slave. After all, a man is in bondage to whatever he cannot part with. Jesus could have taken this man's possessions from him. However, there would have been little benefit to that. Jesus wanted him to voluntarily enter into freedom and life, delivered from the bondage of mammon.

Money is power in this world. This man's possessions gave him a position of importance, which was of value in his eyes. He knew people looked up to him. He liked to be looked up to. He looked up to himself because of his possessions, forgetting that possessions are but tools—and poor tools at that. To part with his wealth would be to sink to the level of his inferiors! Why should he not keep it?

In the final analysis, it is inconceivable that it could be easy for a rich man to enter into the kingdom of heaven. In contrast, there is no kingdom of this world into which a rich man may not easily enter. In fact, if he is rich enough, he can be preeminent in most earthly kingdoms. A kingdom into which it would be easy for a rich man to enter could surely be no kingdom of heaven. I don't mean that the rich man necessarily belongs to the kingdom of Satan. Yet he is especially welcome in Satan's kingdom. However, in the kingdom of heaven he will likely be one of the least—if he is there at all.

To climb the stairway to eternal life, this rich young ruler had to, in effect, throw aside his shoes. He must walk bare-footed into life eternal. However, rather than do so, rather than stride free-limbed up the everlasting stair to the bosom of the Father, he would rather keep his precious shoes! He felt it was better to drag them about on the earth than to part with them for a world where they are useless. But how miserable his precious things—his golden vessels, his embroidered garments, his stately house—must have seemed when he went back to them from the face of the Lord!

What about us? Look at the multitude of professing Christians who are possessed by Things as by a legion of devils? They are in good standing in their churches. Their lives are regarded as spotless. Yet their endless desire is to heap up. To turn the abundance they have into even more. To add house to house and field to field. To bury themselves deeper and deeper in the ash heap of Things.

To be sure, they do not sell Jesus for thirty pieces of silver. On the other hand, they are not willing to buy Him with all that they have! Things can never really be possessed by the person who cannot do without them. The fact that we are unwilling to part with our Things demonstrates that we do not possess them. They possess us. And it is not only the rich who are under the tyranny of Things. Those who are poor, yet are unhappy with their lack of Things, are slaves as well.[71] –George MacDonald

◈◈◈◈◈◈◈◈◈

Why Jesus Taught What He Did

Just as in George MacDonald's day, prosperous modern-day Christians find Jesus' teachings about money and material possessions among His hardest. And so the temptation is to explain away Jesus' words. But if we struggle to obey this commandment, we simply need to be honest about it before God. If we're serious about the Kingdom Life, we need to work to dispossess our souls of material things. For most of us, this is next to impossible in our own power. However, with God's power it can be done.

The starting point is to try to understand *why* Jesus gives us this commandment. Jesus' compelling motive for giving us any command is His deep love for us. So remember that He doesn't give His commandments concerning money and material possessions to be harsh or unkind. He's not trying to make the journey difficult for us. It's just the opposite—He's trying to make the journey feasible for us. He is interested in our eternal welfare.

The reason Jesus bids us to detach ourselves from material things is because it's not possible to serve Him and also pursue riches. He explains, "No servant can serve two masters; for either he will hate the one and love the other, or else he will be loyal to the one and despise the other. You cannot serve God and mammon" (Luke 16:13). Those statements are not a commandment. They're something much stronger. Jesus is stating the facts of Reality—no one can love two things diametrically opposed to each other.

For example, suppose a young Christian man is engaged to a woman. The date of their wedding has already been set. However, he meets another young lady to whom he is more attracted. What can he do? He has to make a choice, doesn't he? He can't have both women. Either he will have to break his engagement to the first woman, or he will have to break off his relationship with the second woman.

It's the same way with Christ and mammon. Most of us are already engaged to mammon when we receive Christ's invitation to follow Him. So we have to break our betrothal to mammon if we want to begin a permanent relationship with Christ. We simply can't have a binding relationship with both. If it were feasible, perhaps Christ would allow us to have both. But it simply is not possible—any more than a man can be betrothed to two different women.

Exclusive Devotion

Producing fruit on the Vine requires a complete commitment to Christ—a commitment that leaves no room for other masters. Even earthly masters often require as much. Shortly after graduating from law school, I was hired by a local company to be their corporate attorney. During the interview, the company president told me that if I accepted the position, this could be my only job. I wouldn't be allowed to take on a part-time job on weekends or evenings. I couldn't try to establish a small law practice on the side—even if it was only "after hours." The company wanted my exclusive devotion, which I agreed to.

I soon learned that there were no "after hours." The company expected to own me. In fact, they not only wanted my body and mind, but my soul as well. The company had to come first—over my private life, my marriage, my church, and anything else that might compete for my heart and soul. It was not a harsh or unpleasant company to work for. However, working there required my complete devotion—devotion no Christian should give to his employer.

If worldly employers can expect exclusive devotion from their key employees, how much more can Jesus expect it from us? There is a big difference, however. Worldly employers demand exclusive devotion for *their* benefit. They aren't thinking of what's best for the employee. In contrast, Jesus requires exclusive devotion for *our* benefit. He doesn't need us; we need Him. He wants us to inherit eternal life, and He realizes there is no other door to it except through complete surrender to Him.

After all, neither Jesus nor His Father has any desire to populate heaven for all eternity with beings who can't appreciate heavenly and eternal things. In the end, heaven is going to be inhabited only by beings who *want* to serve God alone and who will be happy doing so. If you find it miserable right now to give exclusive devotion to Christ, things aren't going to change after you die. If material things attract you now more than spiritual things, it will be that way after the resurrection.

Look at Satan. He had all the eternal things he needed at his fingertips. Yet, even though he was a spirit creature, He found earthly things more attractive than heavenly things. He wanted to possess mankind and the kingdoms of this world instead of eternal things.

Janet, the Diet Coach

Melanie Fudge is fighting obesity. Recently her doctor told her that she is pre-diabetic. He explained to her that this means she is at high risk of developing type-two diabetes. Melanie also has high cholesterol and elevated triglycerides. So she is at increased risk of developing heart disease. Since her health is at risk, Melanie's doctor encouraged her to hire a diet coach to help her control her eating. He recommended Janet Jones.

Following this recommendation, Melanie hired Janet Jones as her diet coach. Janet is both a registered nurse and a certified clinical nutritionist. She has helped numerous clients lose weight. As a result, Melanie has complete confidence in her. At their first meeting, Janet explained that if Melanie is going to lose weight and keep it off, she is going to have to completely change her eating habits. There's no point going on a crash diet to lose weight, because Melanie won't be able to stick to such a diet long term. Permanently losing weight requires a complete lifestyle change.

For this first meeting, Janet had asked Melanie to bring a list of all of the foods in her cupboards, refrigerator, and freezer. After reviewing the list, Janet gently but firmly explained to Melanie that all of the cookies, chips, candy, ice cream, soda, chocolate bars, white bread, pasta, hot dogs, and a number of other foods would have to go. Not surprisingly, Melanie protested that she couldn't possibly live without those things. Janet explained the reality of things: She will have a hard time losing weight if she continues to eat those kinds of food. And if her cupboards and refrigerator are stocked with those foods, she will find it nearly impossible to resist them. Melanie's health—and life—are at stake.

It's no different with Christ. Referring to the parable of the sower, Jesus explains, "He who received seed among the thorns is he who hears the word, but the cares of this world and the deceitfulness of riches choke the word, and he becomes unfruitful" (Matt. 13:22). So Jesus' interest here is that we don't forfeit eternal life because of the "deceitfulness of riches." That's why He bids us again and again to dispossess ourselves of our wealth and not to chase after money and material possessions.

The story of the incompatibility of riches and the Kingdom Life has been written in the sad lives of millions of Christians. During the first three hundred years of Christianity, the vast majority of Christians were poor and many were slaves. Yet they were alive and vigorous spiritually. Living the Kingdom Life was the norm, not the exception. However, once Christianity was legalized and became respectable—even desirable—the situation changed almost overnight. The wealthy and powerful flocked to the church, and eventually controlled it. Within a generation, living the Kingdom Life went from being the norm to being the exception.

The principle has been the same with spiritual movements through the centuries. When the members of a new spiritual movement are mainly poor, embracing the Kingdom Life is common. However, once the members put down roots and begin to prosper, spiritual apathy sets in. This happened with the Mennonites in Holland, the New England Pilgrims, the Quakers, and the Moravians. They were all members of spiritual movements with incredible energy and a strong spirit of self-sacrifice. Yet as soon as material prosperity came to those groups, their lights dimmed.

Jesus isn't being harsh or purposefully trying to make things difficult for us. He knows how Reality works, and He cares about our eternal good. But what exactly did Jesus mean when He said, "Whoever of you does not forsake all that he has cannot be My disciple"?

36

Does This Mean *No* Possessions?

Set your purpose to gain no more. I charge you in the name of God: do not increase your estate! –John Wesley

When Jesus says that we have to forsake all we have, does He mean we cannot own *any* possessions? We want to always take Jesus' words at face value unless the context suggests otherwise. So let's look at the context of Jesus' directive. In the very same passage where He says we must forsake all we have, Jesus also says that in order to be His disciple, a person has to "hate his father and mother, wife and children, brothers and sisters, yes, and his own life also" (Luke 14:26). Yet in the Sermon on the Mount, Jesus says we must love even our enemies. If it's wrong to hate our enemies, how much more so to hate our parents, wives, and children.

So I think it's spiritually and intellectually honest to say that Jesus doesn't mean that we can own absolutely no possessions, anymore than He is saying we must literally hate our spouses. He is saying that, in order to be His disciples, absolutely nothing can be more important in our lives than Him. He has to come ahead of not only our possessions, but even our spouses and children. We have to dispossess all of these things from our souls if they interfere with following Christ.

This meaning is apparent when we read the passage that follows the conversation with the rich young ruler. After the young man left, Peter declared, "We have left all and followed You" (Matt. 19:27). Yet Peter had a wife and home (Matt. 8:14). Surely his home contained a bed, table, and other furniture. No doubt Peter and his wife owned cooking utensils and other such things. So the apostles never understood Jesus to be saying that we can't have any possessions whatsoever.

Jesus' special friends, Martha and Mary, owned a house. Yet Jesus never told them they had to get rid of it (Luke 10:38). Zacchaeus promised to give half of his wealth away and to restore fourfold anything he had taken by false accusation. But he still retained a considerable amount of his wealth. Nevertheless, Jesus declared, "Today salvation has come to this house" (Luke 19:9).

Throughout Acts, we read of various believers who owned houses. We read that they broke bread "from house to house" (Acts 2:46). The apostles preached daily in the temple and "in every house" (Acts 5:42). Peter lodged at the house of Simon the tanner, who presumably was a believer (Acts 10:6). When the angel freed Peter from prison, he went to the "house of Mary, the mother of John whose surname was Mark, where many were gathered together praying" (Acts 12:12). In his letters, Paul makes frequent references to churches that were meeting in the homes of believers.[72] Finally, we read of Christians in the New Testament who not only owned houses, but also owned slaves (Eph. 6:5-9; Col. 4:1).

Dispossessing Things From Our Soul

Nevertheless, we don't want to minimize what Jesus commanded. I think we can accurately say that Jesus did not mean His words in an absolutely literal sense—that is, that we can't own any property whatsoever. But He intended for His words to be taken very seriously. Zacchaeus didn't rid himself of all his property, but He did give away most of it. In the Book of Acts, we read of various Christians owning houses. Yet we also read that "all who were possessors of lands or houses sold them, and brought the proceeds of the things that were sold, and laid them at the apostles' feet; and they distributed to each as anyone had need" (Acts 4:34-35).

Nor should we forget that Paul writes: "Now godliness with contentment is great gain. For we brought nothing into this world, and it is certain we can carry nothing out. And having food and clothing, with these we shall be content. But those who desire to be rich fall into temptation and a snare, and into many foolish and harmful lusts which drown men in destruction and perdition. For the love of money is a root of all kinds of evil, for which some have strayed from the faith in their greediness, and pierced themselves through with many sorrows" (1 Tim 6:6-10).

When it comes to talking about dispossessing our souls of things, the human tendency is to think about everyone who owns more than we do. *They* need to do something about their possessions. But if a person only earns enough to qualify for the bottom rung of the lower middle class in the United States, he or she is still in the top two percent of all earners worldwide.[73]

The rich young ruler was not willing to sell everything he had to follow Jesus. But he would have been more than happy to sell everything he had to change places with most of *us*. We have far more comforts and marvels than he ever dreamed of. So rather than comparing ourselves to someone who earns more than us, we need to focus on the beams in our own eyes. Some of those brothers and sisters who have more than us are quietly helping the poor and building up the kingdom in ways we don't realize. That's because they don't blow trumpets to advertise what they're doing.

So What Can We Do?

The battle to rid our souls of material possessions is not easy. It's much easier to never climb up the ladder of materialism than to have climbed it and now have to climb back down.

For the first few years after I left home, I could fit everything I owned in the back seat of my ten-year-old, beat-up Volkswagen beetle. Serving the Lord was my primary desire, and I was perfectly happy. I see many young Christians today in similar situations. While they're young and single, they're quite content to own little. They're often involved in missions or other ministries. However, something happens to nearly all of us once we get married. Suddenly we want possessions—the more, the better.

Some of this is perfectly legitimate. With children we do need a larger place to live and more furniture. But something seems to happen to our perspective on things. Here in the United States, most couples want to start living the "American dream." My dictionary defines the American dream as "a life of personal happiness and material comfort."[74]

Sadly, the pursuit of "material comfort" is never-ending. A smaller house gives way to a larger one. Older appliances give way to more modern ones. Things of the kingdom get pushed more and more into the background. Soon a young couple is going into debt to purchase things they lack the money to buy. They start viewing certain items as necessities, even though they viewed those same items as luxuries not that long ago. Before long, they are owned by Things. Things dictate how long the husband works each week. Things control how much time he and his wife have for prayer and devotional reading. Things have become their master.

Living the American Dream nearly always becomes a spiritual nightmare. Jesus gets pushed farther and farther into the corner. As I said, it's a lot easier to never start living the American Dream than to have to come down from it. Nevertheless, it is possible to come down the ladder. And we can always count on Jesus' help to do so.

Coming Down the Ladder

I mentioned the fact that for many Christians the idea of living the American Dream doesn't start until after marriage. Coming down the ladder will be significantly easier if both husband and wife are committed to it. Couples should talk about it together and work out a mutual plan if at all possible. If our spouse isn't ready to come down the ladder, we can still do our part in coming down personally.

The first step in coming down the ladder is to simply STOP. Stop accumulating more possessions. Stop thinking about new things to purchase. Stop reading catalogs, advertisements, and magazines that will make you want to purchase new or more glitzy things. Stop exposing yourself to anything—people, magazines, malls, or media—that tends to make you dissatisfied with the things you have. Here are some other suggestions:

- Limit recreational shopping. That is, rarely go into a store unless you're going to buy a specific item that you need.
- When you go shopping, particularly grocery shopping, make up a list ahead of time and stick to

it when you're at the store. This will keep you from impulse buying.

- If you don't have the money for something, don't buy it. If your refrigerator breaks down and you can't afford a new one, perhaps you can pay cash for a reconditioned one or for one with less features.

- Unless you're the rare person who can absolutely control his credit card spending, always use cash for your purchases, unless you're buying online. I realize that you may be able to earn travel miles or other perks by using a credit card. However, no one is giving you those perks just to be nice. They know people spend more when buying with a credit card than when handing over actual cash.

- Physically dispossess yourself of as many things as possible. How many things do you have that you can give to a poorer brother or sister—or to the poor in general?

- Find a church where it's a virtue to be poor. That may sound like a strange statement, but the atmosphere in most conventional churches is one of "keeping up with the Jones." When most of the Christians with whom you fellowship are materialistic, it's going to be hard for you to dispossess your soul of Things.

- Follow Jesus' commandment that when you invite others to dine with you, invite the "poor, the maimed, the lame, and the blind" (Luke 14:13). They will certainly not make you materially envious.

In one of his sermons, John Wesley described one of the early Methodists who was also his close friend and spiritual confidante. When Wesley first came to know this young man, the man had an annual income from his parents' estate of thirty pounds a year, which was slightly more than what a manual laborer earned. The man lived on twenty-eight pounds and gave away two pounds to the poor. The next year his income increased to sixty pounds per year. However, this young man still lived on twenty-eight pounds, but now he gave away thirty-two pounds to the poor. The third year he received ninety pounds of income and gave away sixty-two pounds. The fourth year he received a hundred and twenty pounds. Yet he still lived as before on twenty-eight pounds. So now he could give ninety-two pounds to the poor.* Imagine the impact if all Christians went through life that way![75]

* This friend did not advertise to others what he was doing. Wesley only knew about it because of the spiritual accountability Wesley and his friend had with each other.

37

Andy and the Monopoly Game

We must fix our minds upon immaterial things, until we clearly perceive that these are no dreams; nay, all things are dreams and shadows beside them. –Henry Scougal

Refrain from much business and you will avoid sin. For those with a lot of business are preoccupied about their earthly affairs instead of serving the Lord. –Hermas

It was the first day of summer vacation, and twelve-year-old Andy Dimwit was hoping to find a summer job. Andy's father, Richard, worked for Applegate Realty selling houses and other properties. Many of the properties listed for sale were vacant. As a result, the grass grew tall in these yards unless someone regularly came and mowed them.

When Andy's father came home at lunch that day, he called Andy into the living room. "Guess what? I asked Mr. Applegate if it was okay to hire you to mow the yards of our vacant properties over the summer."

"What did he say?" Andy asked eagerly, laying aside the book he had been reading.

"He said he was willing to do it on a trial basis. We have a lawn that needs to be mowed right now. I'll be showing the house to some prospective buyers later today, so we need you to mow the lawn this afternoon. It should take you no more than two hours."

"Sounds good!" Andy replied excitedly. "How much will Mr. Applegate pay?"

"He'll pay you fifty dollars. The house is only a block away, so you can walk over there with the lawnmower after lunch." Pulling a slip of paper out of his shirt pocket, Andy's father continued, "Here's the address. You can't miss it, as there's a For Sale sign in front of the house."

Andy beamed. "That's wonderful, Dad. Thanks so much for asking Mr. Applegate for me. I'll get right over there after lunch."

"Make sure you do," Andy's father warned. "I'm not sure what time the buyers are coming. I think it'll be around six o'clock, but it could be as early as four."

"Don't worry. You can count on me."

"I'm sure I can. And if you do a good job on this one, Mr. Applegate will have a lot more mowing jobs for you. You'll be set for the summer."

"Thanks so much, Dad!" Andy replied. As he headed for the stairs, he added: "I'm going to change into my work clothes right now."

Andy finished his lunch around one o'clock and said goodbye to his father, who was leaving. Andy's mom had already left to go shopping. Andy himself was just starting out the front door when he saw his friend Tommy and a group of neighborhood boys coming up the front sidewalk. Tommy held a Monopoly game box under his arm.

"Hi, Andy," Tommy called out. "Guess what? We've come over to play Monopoly."

"Oh, no!" Andy groaned. "I can't play this afternoon. I have to go mow a yard for my dad."

"Oh, that's too bad," Tommy replied. "Are you sure you don't have time for just a quick game? How long will it take you to mow the yard?"

"Hmm," Andy thought for a moment. "It'll take me a couple of hours. But my dad probably won't be showing it until six this evening. I guess we have time for a quick game. Come on in."

The boys followed Andy into the living room, and they sprawled out on the floor.

"I'll be the banker," called out Frank, a red-headed boy a couple of years younger than Andy.

Before long, the boys were into the game. They all ended up with fairly evenly matched properties, so the game moved slowly. Andy kept glancing nervously at the clock on the living room wall. At two o'clock he announced, "Listen, I'm sorry, guys. I hate to quit in the middle of the game, but I've really got to go mow that yard now."

"What! You can't quit now. The game is just getting interesting," one of the boys protested. The others joined in.

"Well, okay," Andy muttered. "But thirty minutes more at the max."

The boys assured him it would be over within thirty minutes. Andy eventually ended up with Boardwalk and Park Place, plus three of the railroads. With these properties, he slowly gained on the other boys. Before long, he was so engrossed in the game that he didn't notice the time. Two-thirty passed. Then three.

When three-thirty rolled around, only Andy and two other boys were left in the game. By four o'clock, Andy had picked up another monopoly and some other valuable properties. He and Tommy were the only players left.

Suddenly the front door flung open, startling the boys. Andy's father stood in the doorway, glaring at Andy. Andy glanced at the clock and saw that it was four-thirty.

"Oh, I forgot the time!" Andy blurted out. "Don't worry, Dad, I'm leaving right now. I'll have it mowed by six."

"I'm afraid it's too late, Andy," his dad countered solemnly. "The people wanted to see it at four, and I've just come back from there. The overgrown lawn didn't make a very good impression, and they decided not to buy the house."

"Oh. I . . . I'm sorry, Dad," Andy offered quietly. "Don't worry. It won't happen next time."

"I'm afraid there won't be a next time, Andy. When he heard what happened, Mr. Applegate decided to give the summer mowing jobs to his nephew Fred. Because of some silly game, you just threw away a golden opportunity to earn some real money this summer."

"But Dad," Andy protested, picking up his Monopoly money in both hands and showing it to his father. "Look! I've won over $8,000! Plus I own Boardwalk and Park Place, with a hotel on each one!"

38

The Point of the Story

If all that is in the world are only so many empty cups, what does it signify which you take, or how many you take, or how many you have? –William Law

Bended knees while you are clothed with pride? Heavenly petitions, while you are hoarding up treasures upon earth? –William Law

True evangelical faith is of such a nature that it cannot lay dormant. It clothes the naked, feeds the hungry, consoles the afflicted, shelters the miserable, and aids and consoles all the oppressed. –Menno Simons

I think we would all agree that Andy Dimwit lives up to his name. "But what does this have to do with me?" you may be wondering. Actually, the story has everything to do with you and me. That's because many—if not most—Christians are basically Andy Dimwits.

Getting a Perspective on Reality

What many people don't grasp is that the instant we die, all of the money we've accumulated on earth turns into Monopoly money. Our houses turn into those little green plastic Monopoly houses. The game is over. Forever.

Of course, these possessions benefit our heirs. But they are of no more use to us. That's why Jesus calls us away from our Monopoly game to do His work. We have a *real* job to do here on earth. However, most of us are so busy gaining Monopoly money and plastic houses that we neglect the real job. In His parable of the minas, Jesus tells us He expects us to be working on His behalf until His return. He says, "A certain nobleman went into a far country to receive for himself a kingdom and to return. So he called ten of his servants, delivered to them ten minas, and said to them, 'Do business till I come' " (Luke 19:12-13). So we are to be 'doing business' for our King until He returns.

In the Sermon on the Mount, Jesus instructed us: "Do not worry, saying, 'What shall we eat?' or 'What shall we drink?' or 'What shall we wear?' For after all these things the Gentiles seek. For your heavenly Father knows that you need all these things. But seek first the kingdom of God and His righteousness, and all these things shall be added to you" (Matt. 6:31-33). So our main focus as Christians is to be seeking Kingdom interests.

Paul exhorted the entire Corinthian church, "My beloved brethren, be steadfast, immovable, always abounding in the work of the Lord, knowing that your labor is not in vain in the Lord" (1 Cor. 15:58). So what is this "work of the Lord" we should be abounding in? What kingdom interests should we be seeking first? What is the Lord's business that He expects us to be engaged in?

What Is Our Kingdom Work?

The New Testament describes numerous types of Kingdom work that we can be doing until our Lord returns. Here are twenty of them: 1) Feeding the hungry,[76] 2) providing drink to the thirsty,[77] 3) providing shelter for travelers and the poor,[78] 4) clothing the needy,[79] 5) calling on the sick,[80] 6) visiting ones in prison,[81] 7) preaching the gospel of the kingdom,[82] 8) church planting,[83] 9) teaching in the church,[84] 10) serving in church leadership,[85] 11) mentoring and discipling other Christians,[86] 12) ministering to and supporting those serving as leaders, evangelists, and missionaries,[87] 13) interceding in prayer,[88] 14) being a peacemaker,[89] 15) comforting others,[90] 16) showing hospitality to travelers and kingdom workers,[91] 17) administrating churches and ministries,[92] 18) caring for widows and orphans,[93] 19) being an encourager,[94] and 20) using gifts of the Spirit to advance the kingdom.[95]

In addition to those kingdom services, many Christians today serve in ministries like Bible translation, giving medical care to the sick, curing diseases, teaching improved agricultural methods to farmers, publishing Christian literature, organizing and serving at Christian conferences, cleaning and maintaining church buildings, volunteering to regularly babysit, providing microloans to the poor, helping people break addictions, caring for new mothers, and providing shelters for the homeless and abused.

Probably most Christians spend some time in these types of ministries or support them through donations. However, to live the Kingdom Life these ministries have to come *first* in our lives. In saying that, I don't mean that we necessarily spend more time in these ministries than at our jobs or homemaking. I mean that such kingdom service must be our vocation.

What Is Your Vocation?

When it comes to work, Jesus instructs us, "Do not labor for the food which perishes, but for the food which endures to everlasting life" (John 6:27). So which food are we primarily laboring for? The kind that perishes or the kind that "endures to everlasting life"? Those living the Kingdom Life already have a vocation—serving the Kingdom of God. This is the highest vocation on earth.

The early Christians never referred to their jobs and businesses as their vocations. Their vocation was serving God and His Kingdom. Clement of Alexandria writes,

"If, through the necessity of life, he spends a small portion of time for his sustenance, the spiritual man thinks himself defrauded, being diverted by business."[96]

The Right Use of Secular Work

Am I suggesting, then, that a Christian shouldn't have a job? Not at all. The New Testament teachings on secular work are quite clear. Paul wrote, "For you yourselves know how you ought to follow us, for we were not disorderly among you; nor did we eat anyone's bread free of charge, but worked with labor and toil night and day, that we might not be a burden to any of you, not because we do not have authority, but to make ourselves an example of how you should follow us. For even when we were with you, we commanded you this: If anyone will not work, neither shall he eat. For we hear that there are some who walk among you in a disorderly manner, not working at all, but are busybodies. Now those who are such we command and exhort through our Lord Jesus Christ that they work in quietness and eat their own bread" (2 Thess. 3:7-12).

So part of our service to God is to provide for our own material needs and the needs of our families. As the Scriptures say, "Let him who stole steal no longer, but rather let him labor, working with his hands what is good" (Eph. 4:28). Christians should not be a burden to their church or to the public if they have the ability to work with their hands and provide for themselves. Not only that, jobs and businesses enable us to provide for those who are in need. But it is easy to let our earthly work—whether it's a job outside the home or homemaking—become the central focus of our energy. It's easy to whittle away our time here on earth accumulating Monopoly money and green plastic houses.

Now let's return to Jesus' instructions to the rich young ruler. Jesus told him not only to sell what he had, but also to "give to the poor." But is giving to the poor really that important? Surely it's not a salvation issue—or is it?

39

How to Make Friends With Stolen Money

Love poverty and reverence poor people. For our Blessed Savior was one of their number, and you may make them all so many friends and advocates with God for you. –William Law

When Mortimer Sly was a boy, his parents and teachers all told him he would never amount to anything. And they were right. He frittered away his time in school and barely finished high school. From the time he was a toddler, Mortimer had been a clumsy, awkward lad. Once he was out of school, he tried to learn various trades, but he could never quite get a handle on any of them. The fact that he was incredibly lazy and undependable didn't help matters any.

Happily for Mortimer, he had a rich uncle who took a liking to him. Nobody can quite figure out what Uncle Nick saw in Mortimer, but Uncle Nick had no children of his own, so he looked upon his nephew as a son. Uncle Nick was the president and chief stockholder of Middleton Savings and Loan. His company held nearly a quarter of the home mortgages in the small town of Middleton.

Taking pity on Mortimer, one day Uncle Nick gave him a nice cushy desk job at his savings and loan. In fact, in his generosity, he made Mortimer a vice-president in the company, hoping that someday Mortimer could succeed him as president. But Mortimer never made much effort to learn the savings and loan business. He took long coffee breaks, played computer games when he should have been working, and distracted the other employees with his constant chatter.

Things went downhill from there. On a number of occasions, Mortimer neglected to file important paperwork, costing the company penalties and fines. He often charged personal expenses on his business account and took unauthorized loans. Finally, his uncle had had enough.

"Mortimer, I really wanted to give you a chance in life by giving you this job," Uncle Nick began. "We both knew you weren't qualified, but I hoped you would apply yourself and learn the mortgage business. Instead you've played around and never made the slightest effort to learn the workings of the company. Your neglect, wastefulness, and outright dishonesty have cost the company tens of thousands of dollars. I had fondly hoped that someday you might replace me, but you've proved yourself utterly unworthy of such hopes. I'm terminating your position in thirty days."

"But Uncle Nick, what will I do? I have no college education and no job skills," Mortimer protested.

"I'm sorry, but you should have thought about that when you neglected your duties here. I gave you a once-in-a-lifetime opportunity, and you flung it back in my face."

Mortimer went home that night visibly shaken. He lay awake most of the night wondering what he would do. If only he had some other connections in town. But he had none. There was no one he could turn to for help . . . unless . . .

I have access to all the mortgage files, Mortimer suddenly realized. *I have the authority to adjust mortgages, mark them paid, and release them*. He now grasped that he was in a great position to do some big favors.

Mortimer showed up at the office as usual the next morning, but he left work early—with a briefcase full of mortgage documents. Instead of going home, he dropped by the restaurant owned by Enrico Rossi. Mortimer greeted Mr. Rossi as he was shown into his office.

"Hello, Mr. Sly," Enrico answered nervously. "I, uh . . . I think I know why you're here. Listen, I know we're past due on our mortgage payments. But business is slow right now, and, uh, we've had some unexpected medical expenses . . ."

"No, no," Mortimer reassured him, smiling. "That's not why I'm here. Well, at least I'm not here to talk to you about your late payments. The reason I'm here is that my uncle has just put me in charge of helping our distressed borrowers. I've started a new program for families in situations like yours."

Enrico's eyes lit up. "Yeah? Tell me more."

"Well, here's how it works. Right now you owe $41,380 on your mortgage. Since it's past due, we could declare it all due and payable right now. However, if you can somehow scrape together a tenth of that amount—$4,138—I'll mark the entire mortgage paid and release the deed of trust."

"You can't be serious!" Enrico answered.

"I assure you that I am."

"But where would I get $4,138? I'm broke."

"Don't you have family or friends who might loan it to you?"

"You're right," Enrico announced confidently. "I think my wife's parents will help us. But are you really serious? I pay $4,138, and you'll mark the entire mortgage as paid off? Ten cents on the dollar?"

"I couldn't be more serious," Mortimer replied. "Can you get it to me by the end of next week?"

"I'm pretty sure I can," Enrico answered. "I'll see you then." As Mortimer walked out the door, Enrico added, "Hey, listen. Anytime you want a meal, just come to my restaurant. It'll be on the house. Come as often as you want."

"Well, thanks," Mortimer replied with a smile. "I'm sure I'll take you up on that."

Over the next couple of days, Mortimer cut similar deals with Bob Ingram, Wally Goff, and Alicia Martinez. Bob owned a hardware store, Wally owned an auto garage, and Alicia was a retired widow. Bob promised Mortimer a job in his store if he ever needed one. Wally told Mortimer he could bring in his car anytime to be repaired for free. And Alicia promised he could live rent-free in the empty apartment above her garage if he ever needed a place to stay. Mortimer was all set.

After all these mortgages had been released under the special terms granted by Mortimer, Uncle Nick found out about them. He burst into Mortimer's office one morning without knocking. "I've been doing some inquiring, and I've found out about the deals you cut with Enrico Rossi and the others."

Mortimer gulped, dreading what was about to come. But to his great surprise, his uncle smiled broadly and said, "You know, that's the smartest thing you've done since you came to work for me. I'm glad to see you're finally using your head." With that, Uncle Nick walked out the door, quietly closing it behind him.

What About Reality?

You're probably thinking, "That's the most outlandish yarn I've ever heard. It's not even remotely plausible. If you're going to make up an illustration, at least come up with one that's believable!"

Well, yes, you're right. This story is simply too flaky to be believable. In fact, now that I think about it, it's beyond fiction. It's in the realm of fantasy.

Except for one thing. It happens to be true.

I don't mean that Mortimer, Uncle Nick, and Enrico Rossi are real people. I mean that this story happens in the Real universe. In fact, you probably recognize this story as a modern adaptation of Jesus' parable of the unjust steward, recorded in Luke 16. Uncle Nick represents God the Father. He allows us to give *His* property away to others and then turns around and commends us for doing it! In fact, He not only commends us, but He says we will be given an eternal home for giving His property away.

What does all this mean in real life? It means that everything we think we possess on earth is really God's. Even though we work hard to acquire the money and material possessions we have, we're using resources that actually belong to God. We've already talked about the fact that without the resources God provides, the farmer could grow nothing. Think of how many millions of people on earth besides farmers earn their living through agriculture. Picture the people who work in grocery stores, restaurants, food processing, canning factories, bakeries, butcher shops, pet food factories, feed stores, and so many other places connected with the food industry.

What about the millions of people who earn their living from products that come from petroleum—products like gasoline, plastics, paint, fertilizer, carpets, roofing materials, tires, Styrofoam, synthetic fabrics, solvents, linoleum, anesthetics, eyeglasses, insecticides, and thousands of other products. Think of how many industries depend upon trees: logging, carpentry, furniture making, forestry, lumberyards, paper mills, newspapers, book publishers, print shops, pencil factories, and cellulose production—just to name a few. Similar things can be said about jobs connected with fishing, metals, water, solar power, chemicals, medicines, minerals, and wind.

In the end, few people can earn a living without either directly or indirectly using the materials that God has created. Yet no one pays God one cent for these resources. We've accumulated our possessions using *His* resources. So when we give to the poor, we're actually giving His money to the poor, not our own. Yet the poor are grateful to *us* for giving them *God's* money. And God turns around and rewards us for the "dishonest" thing we've done. It's exactly like Mortimer Sly and his benefactors. What is too absurd to be true in earthly things is precisely real in the realm of eternity.

Listen to What Jesus Says

This time I want you to hear the story from Jesus' own lips:

> There was a certain rich man who had a steward, and an accusation was brought to him that this man was wasting his goods. So he called him and said to him, "What is this I hear about you? Give an account of your stewardship, for you can no longer be steward."
>
> Then the steward said within himself, "What shall I do? For my master is taking the stewardship away from me. I cannot dig; I am ashamed to beg. I have resolved what to do, that when I am put out of the stewardship, they may receive me into their houses."

> So he called every one of his master's debtors to him, and said to the first, "How much do you owe my master?" And he said, "A hundred measures of oil." So he said to him, "Take your bill, and sit down quickly and write fifty." Then he said to another, "And how much do you owe?" So he said, "A hundred measures of wheat." And he said to him, "Take your bill, and write eighty." So the master commended the unjust steward because he had dealt shrewdly. For the sons of this world are more shrewd in their generation than the sons of light.
>
> And I say to you, make friends for yourselves by unrighteous mammon, that when you fail, they may receive you into an everlasting home. Luke 16:1-10

Like many other Christians, I had read this parable a number of times. However, it never meant much to me. It seemed a strange parable without any clear application. In fact, I remember once hearing a sermon about it. When the preacher reached the final sentence—where Jesus explains the whole point of the parable—he rushed through the words: "I say to you, make friends for yourselves by unrighteous mammon, that when you fail, they may receive you into an everlasting home." The preacher brushed these words aside by shrugging and commenting, "I have no idea what that's all about."

I certainly didn't have a clue either until I read the early Christian writings. The early Christians talked about this parable a lot. To them the meaning was obvious: We can take God's money and use it to help the poor. Because of our kindness to them with money that's not ours to begin with, we will be received in eternal homes when both our lives and our possessions fail us.

This shouldn't sound strange, for Jesus essentially says the same thing in His description of Judgment Day, when He separates the sheep from the goats. The only criteria He mentions in that description are whether or not we fed the hungry, gave drink to the thirsty, clothed the naked, took in the stranger, and visited the sick and imprisoned. He says:

> Then the King will say to those on His right hand, "Come, you blessed of My Father, inherit the kingdom prepared for you from the foundation of the world: for I was hungry and you gave Me food; I was thirsty and you gave Me drink; I was a stranger and you took Me in; I was naked and you clothed Me; I was sick and you visited Me; I was in prison and you came to Me." Matt. 25:34-36

I remember the first time I preached a sermon about the parable of the unjust steward. I don't think I've ever seen so many furrowed brows and faces expressing disbelief. A person would have thought I had made up this parable myself. That was the first of many similar experiences when I have preached the same message that Jesus preached.

I have to admit that when I first read what the early Christian writers said about this parable, I had trouble accepting it. Teachers, authors, and preachers had drummed into my mind that giving alms has nothing to do with salvation. In fact, for a person to even talk about "giving alms" makes his orthodoxy suspect. "We are justified by faith *alone*," we've all heard over and over. But nowhere in Scripture does it say we are saved by faith alone. In fact, the Bible expressly says just the opposite: "You see then that a man is justified by works, and not by faith only" (Jas. 2:24). *Martin Luther* said we are justified by faith alone. Jesus did not. Whom are we going to believe?

40

The Sympathetic College Professor

God is love, and He has no pleasure in the ruin of His creatures. –Henry Scougal

Dr. Rod Wyse teaches history at Greensburg State University. Every semester he ends up having to give failing grades to a number of his students. Some university professors might enjoy failing some of their students, but not Professor Wyse. He tries his hardest to convey the information in his lectures, but somehow a large number of students perform poorly on his final exams.

Feeling sympathy for his students, one semester, a week before the final exam, he decides to do something he has never done before: He will tell his students in advance what the questions are going to be on the final exam. Not only that, he'll even tell them the answers he's looking for. "For once," Dr. Wyse says to himself, "I'll have nothing but A's on the final exam."

So a week before the exam, Dr. Wyse hands out a set of stapled pages to each student. "These are the exact questions that will be on the final exam—plus the precise answers I want you to give," he explains.

As you can imagine, the students all sit there with their mouths wide open. They stare at one another in disbelief. "Are you serious?" one of the students asks incredulously.

"Yes, I'm quite serious," the professor responds. "For once, I want to see every one of you pass the exam. In fact, I want every one of you to get an A. However, you won't be allowed to bring these questions and answers with you into the exam room. You will have to study them and know the answers by heart."

A week later, Dr. Wyse gives the exam. When it is over, he stacks the finished tests neatly and carries them to his office, excited that for once everyone will pass. However, when he grades the first paper, he discovers that the student gave the wrong answers for most of the questions. He shakes his head in bewilderment. What happened? *Maybe this student was sick or something,* he thinks.

However, when he gets to the next paper, he finds that this student also missed a lot of the questions and just barely passed. Dr. Wyse moves to the third paper. But the third student missed many questions as well. When Dr. Wyse finishes grading all of the exams, he finds that just as many students failed as on past exams. Out of his whole class, only three or four students made A's. What could have gone wrong?

When the next semester starts, Dr. Wyse is walking to his office one day when he sees Susan, one of his students from the prior semester. "Oh, hi Susan," he begins. "Listen, I'm wondering if you can clear up a mystery for me."

"Well, I'll try," Susan responds with a smile. "What's this mystery?"

"It's this," Dr. Wyse answers. "As you remember, last semester, a week before the finals, I gave everyone in the class a handout containing all the questions that would be on the final exam, plus all of the correct answers. Naturally, I assumed the whole class would make A's since they had the questions and answers in advance. Yet only you and a couple of other students made A's.

"Really?" Susan replies. "I didn't realize that."

"Yes, that's the sad truth," Dr. Wyse continues. "There were a number of C's and D's—and even some F's. Do you have any idea what happened?"

Susan thought for a moment. "You know, I think I do know what happened. Right after your class, a lot of us were eating lunch at the student union and talking about your exam. It was hard to believe that you really would tell us in advance the questions and answers. Luther Little had a theory. He said, 'I'm guessing that old Dr. Wyse is trying to trick us. Think about it. Would a professor really give his students the questions and answers for the final exam? He would probably get in trouble with the university.' "

"What did the other students say?" Dr. Wyse asked.

"Well, the conversation went back and forth. But eventually most of the students agreed with Luther. The theory was that you wanted us to look past the answers you gave us—to dig deeper and get down to the *real* answers. So most of the students met that night and tried to figure out the real answers for themselves."

"Did you join them?" the professor asked.

"No, I didn't," Susan replied. "I got thinking to myself, 'Is that what I really think of Dr. Wyse? Is he so mean that he would try to trick us? Can I really believe that he *wants* to flunk us? What kind of person would do that?' So after thinking it over, I decided to believe you. I studied the questions and answers you gave us."

The Real Dr. Wyse

Like the story about Mortimer Sly, this story about Dr. Wyse also happens to be true. The names and setting have obviously been changed. But the story is real. Our

Teacher, Jesus Christ, has told us what the exam questions are going to be on Judgment Day. The questions will be, "Did you feed the hungry, give drink to the thirsty, clothe the naked, and visit those who were sick or imprisoned?" There's only one correct answer: Yes. And Jesus will already know whether or not we have done these things before we stand in front of Him.

How easy could Christ possibly make it for us? He gives us both the questions and answers in advance. And this is no mere college exam. It's our eternal destiny. Yet Christians do the exact same thing that Luther Little did in my story. They decide that Jesus isn't going to judge us based on anything we have done. Therefore, we can safely ignore His words. Just last week, I was reading a Christian pamphlet in which the author asserted, "Remember one and all that there is NOTHING we can DO to get into heaven."[97]

The author is correct that there is nothing we can do to *earn* our salvation. It will always be a gift to those with a living faith who produce godly fruit. However, a faith that produces no fruit is not saving faith.

A Theme Throughout the Gospels

Matthew 25 is so clear about Judgment Day that there's no way we could quibble with it even if Jesus never said anything further on the subject. However, rarely does any foundational teaching of Christianity rest on just one New Testament passage. And Jesus' teaching about helping the poor is no exception. The theme of helping the poor runs throughout His ministry and the New Testament. Here are a few examples:

- The parable of the unjust steward (Luke 16:1-13).

- The story of the rich man and Lazarus (Luke 16:19-31).
- "Give to him who asks you, and from him who wants to borrow from you do not turn away" (Matt. 5:42).
- "When you do a charitable deed, do not let your left hand know what your right hand is doing, that your charitable deed may be in secret; and your Father who sees in secret will Himself reward you openly" (Matt. 6:3-4). (Please note that Jesus says *when* you do a charitable deed, not *if* you do one.)
- "Blessed are you poor, for yours is the kingdom of God" (Luke 6:20).
- "Sell what you have and give alms; provide yourselves money bags which do not grow old, a treasure in the heavens that does not fail, where no thief approaches nor moth destroys" (Luke 12:33).
- "But when you give a feast, invite the poor, the maimed, the lame, [and] the blind" (Luke 14:13).
- "Then Zacchaeus stood and said to the Lord, 'Look, Lord, I give half of my goods to the poor; and if I have taken anything from anyone by false accusation, I restore fourfold.' And Jesus said to him, 'Today salvation has come to this house' " (Luke 19:8,9).

The same message resonates throughout the rest of the New Testament. In Acts, the angel tells Cornelius, "Your prayers and your alms have come up for a memorial before God" (Acts 10:4). Describing his meeting with the leaders of the Jerusalem church, Paul writes: "When James, Cephas, and John, who seemed to be pillars, perceived the grace that had been given to me, they gave me and Barnabas the right hand of fellowship, that we should go to the Gentiles and they to the circumcised. They desired *only that we should remember the poor,* the very thing which I also was eager to do" (Gal. 2:9-10, italics mine).

Helping the poor is more than just a commendable thing to do. Jesus and His disciples tell us that it is essential to the Christian life. James writes, "This is pure and undefiled religion in the sight of our God and Father, to visit orphans and widows in their distress" (Jas. 1:27 NAS). James goes on to say that refusal to help the poor is an example of dead faith: "If a brother or sister is naked and destitute of daily food, and one of you says to them, 'Depart in peace, be warmed and filled,' but you do not give them the things which are needed for the body, what does it profit? Thus also faith by itself, if it does not have works, is dead" (Jas. 2:15-16).

Although many Christians imagine Paul teaches salvation through a once-and-done faith, he says the opposite. He shows that our faith must be enduring, and it must produce fruit: "Command those who are rich in this present age not to be haughty, nor to trust in uncertain riches but in the living God, who gives us richly all things to enjoy. Let them do good, that they be rich in good works, ready to give, willing to share, storing up for themselves a good foundation for the time to come, *that they may lay hold on eternal life*" (1 Tim. 6:17-19 italics mine).

Does that mean we can buy our way into heaven? Let's see.

41

Turning Monopoly Money Into Real Money

Every penny you save from your own wardrobe you may expend in clothing the naked and relieving the needs of the poor. –John Wesley

Every pound you put into the earthly bank is sunk, for it brings no interest above. But every pound you give to the poor is put into the bank of heaven. – John Wesley

Andy never did find a summer job, so he spent just about every afternoon playing Monopoly with his friends. One day while Andy and his friends were engrossed in a game, Andy's father came home unexpectedly in the middle of the afternoon. His eyes were shining, and he was wearing a tremendous smile.

"Andy, you're not going to believe what I'm about to tell you," he began. "But I've been telling Mr. Applegate how you and your friends play Monopoly every afternoon."

"And he disapproves, right?" Andy interjected.

"No. That's not it at all. Instead, he just now told me that regardless of where you are in your Monopoly game this afternoon, he will trade real dollars for whatever Monopoly money you have won so far. Listen to this next part, because it sounds unbelievable, but he will trade you *dollar for dollar*. One dollar of real money for one dollar of Monopoly money!"

"What!" Andy exclaimed in disbelief. "That doesn't make any sense. You're saying that he will give me real U.S. dollars for my Monopoly dollars? That's crazy!"

"I know it sounds crazy, but that's exactly what he'll do. I was just like you. I was sure he was just kidding, but he assured me that he's not."

"But why? Why would he do that?" Andy asked.

"He assured me he has his reasons," Andy's father replied. "But quit worrying about why he's doing it. How much money do you have in your hand right now?"

"Well, I don't know. I'll have to count it." Andy counted his money hurriedly. "It comes to $4,176," he announced.

"Fine," his father said. "Now tell me how many houses and hotels you have. You can sell them to the bank for half of what you paid for them."

"Dad, you don't understand," Andy protested. "For the first time in the past two weeks, I'm finally ahead in a game. I own the yellow monopoly, which pays really well. And I'm close to picking up a second monopoly. I don't own any hotels yet, but I do have four houses on each of the yellow properties. If I sell my houses back to the bank, I'll only get half of what I paid for them. Plus, if I do that, I'll lose all the income I would otherwise get from the yellow monopoly. I could end up losing the game!"

"What do you mean, you'll lose the game?" Andy's father exclaimed. "I'm talking about *real* money here! Mr. Applegate will give you several thousand dollars for your silly Monopoly money. Aren't you listening?"

"Yes, I hear what you're saying. But you must not be hearing what *I'm* saying. I haven't won at Monopoly in several weeks, and now I have my big chance." Andy paused. "All right, suppose I take Mr. Applegate up on his offer. Will I get the money today?"

"No, not today. Mr. Applegate said that if you give him the Monopoly money today, he'll give you the cash at the end of summer—two months from now."

Andy was dumbstruck. "Two months!" he finally shouted. "Of course not! You mean I lose my Monopoly game today, but I don't get any benefit for two whole months? Dad, that's ridiculous."

Andy's friends all chimed in, joining his side. "That's the stupidest offer I've ever heard," one of them barked, rolling his eyes. "Who but an idiot would accept an offer like that?"

So Andy kept his Monopoly money, his green plastic houses, and his cardboard deeds.

Oh, by the way, he *did* win that Monopoly game.

Jesus' Offer

Jesus makes us an offer similar to that of Mr. Applegate. Only His offer is much, much better. He offers to exchange our earthly Monopoly money for eternal money. He invites us to "make friends for yourselves by unrighteous mammon, that when you fail, they may receive you into an everlasting home" (Luke 16:9). He bids us to "lay up for yourselves treasures in heaven" (Matt. 6:20).

So how do we exchange Monopoly money for real money? How do we convert temporal, earthly money into eternal, heavenly money? It's actually very easy. For example, let's suppose you are planning to buy a used motorboat for $5,000 for recreation. That's basically using Monopoly money to buy a plastic Monopoly object. That same $5,000 can be converted into real, eternal money by using it in one of the following ways, at home or in a developing country:

- It may provide the needed medical care to save someone's life or restore hearing to a deaf person.
- It could support an elderly Christian widow for the rest of her life.
- Over time, it could help put fifty Christians through life by providing microloans to help them start small businesses.
- It could help hundreds or thousands of people hear the gospel message.
- In a developing country, it could put ten Christian students through high school, enabling them to be able to better provide for their families as adults.

The list is endless. Now I used the illustration of a recreational item, but the same principle applies to every purchase we make and to every dollar we put aside for future purchases. One of the secrets of the Kingdom Life is to always be aware of this heavenly conversion table.

The instant we die that $5,000 motorboat is worthless to us. Of course, it still has value to those left behind. But if we used that $5,000 to save the life of a brother or sister, or to bless him in some other way, that person will be thanking us for *all eternity*. If our money made it possible for someone to hear the gospel, be saved, and eventually be in heaven, we have made an eternal friend. If nothing more were at stake than our own personal happiness, making eternal friends with our money would still be the way to go.

However, far more than our personal happiness is as stake. At the end of the parable of the unjust steward, Jesus explained the point of the parable: "He who is faithful in what is least is faithful also in much; and he who is unjust in what is least is unjust also in much. Therefore if you have not been faithful in the unrighteous mammon, who will commit to your trust the true riches? And if you have not been faithful in what is another man's, who will give you what is your own? No servant can serve two masters; for either he will hate the one and love the other, or else he will be loyal to the one and despise the other. You cannot serve God and mammon" (Luke 16:10-13).

If we can't faithfully use our temporary Monopoly money in a way to serve God, then God is not going to entrust us with eternal things. Jesus goes on to point out that all of our assets on earth ultimately are God's assets. If we can't use His assets wisely, then He will never give us eternal ones of our own. We tend to see money and property as big things. Jesus is explaining Reality to us: they are little things. And if we can't be faithful in such a little thing as our use of money, heaven has no place for us. An Andy Dimwit could never appreciate heaven; he could never be at home there.

However, lest we try to buy our way into the kingdom, Paul gives us this warning: "Though I bestow all my goods to feed the poor, and though I give my body to be burned, but have not love, it profits me nothing" (1 Cor. 13:3). So love for others has to be the ultimate motivation behind our giving to the poor. In other words, our care for the poor must be an outpouring of the fruit of love. We can't earn our salvation or buy our way into heaven.

Yes, it is our faith that saves us. But it must be an enduring, living faith that produces fruit—particularly the fruit of love for the poor.

Examples of Living the Kingdom Life

Throughout most of Christian history, no Christians would have dreamed they were living the Kingdom Life unless they were helping the poor and visiting the sick and imprisoned. In the second century, Tertullian pointed out to the Romans, "Our compassion spends more in the streets than yours does in the temples!"[98] He went on to explain the many ways Christians in his day helped the poor:

> These gifts go to support and bury poor people, to supply the needs of boys and girls destitute of means and of parents, and to aid old persons who are now confined to the house. These gifts also help those who have suffered shipwreck. And if there happens to be any of us in the mines, or banished to the islands, or shut up in the prisons—for no reason other than their faithfulness to the cause of God's Church—they become the nurslings of their confession.[99]

In the fourth century after Christianity had become the dominant religion, the Roman emperor Julian tried to restore the pagan religions throughout the empire. However, one reason his efforts met with little success was because Christians were so diligent in helping the poor. Julian lamented, "The sacrilegious Christians support not only their own poor but ours as well."[100]

For most of my life, I've heard of the city of St. Louis. However, until recently I had no idea who the man was it was named after. It turns out that St. Louis was a French king of the High Middle Ages who tried to live the Kingdom Life. To be sure, King Louis didn't understand certain aspects of kingdom living, such as the doctrine of the two kingdoms. However, with the knowledge he did have, he lived as close to Christ as possible. Although a king, every day he personally brought food to houses of the poor and served them in other ways. Each day he invited various beggars to come and eat with him at his own table. He would often let them fill their plates first, and he would eat what was left over. He frequently visited hospitals, where he would call on those afflicted with the most loathsome diseases. He then knelt down at their beds, washing them and tenderly caring for their abscesses and sores.[101]

I've quoted William Law many times in this book. He, along with two elderly ladies, the single Hester Gibbon and the widowed Mrs. Hutcheson, lived the Kingdom Life to the full. They pooled their collective incomes and lived on a tenth of the total. They gave the remaining ninety percent to the poor. In the English village of King's Cliffe where they lived, every morning poor people lined up outside their doors for aid, which they gave freely. In addition, these three used some of the ninety percent to establish free schools for poor girls and boys. They also established almshouses where the poor and elderly could live for nothing.[102]

I want to close our discussion of caring for the poor with one last story. It's a true story about John Wesley that he shared in one of his sermons. I'll let him tell it:

> Many years ago, when I was at Oxford, on a cold winter's day, a young maid (one of those we kept at the school) called upon me. I said, "You seem half-starved. Have you nothing to cover you but that thin linen gown?"
>
> She said, "Sir, this is all I have!"
>
> I put my hand in my pocket, but I found I had no money left, having just spent what I had on some pretty pictures for my wall. It immediately struck me, "John Wesley, will your Master say, 'Well done, good and faithful servant?' No, indeed. For you have adorned your walls with the money that might have protected this poor creature from the cold![103]

In Wesley's day, wall pictures were not as affordable as they are today. Wesley concluded his sermon with these words: "How often have you prevented yourself from doing good by purchasing that which you did not need?"[104]

42

Truly Appreciating Grace

What then? Shall we sin because we are not under law but under grace? Certainly not! Do you not know that to whom you present yourselves slaves to obey, you are that one's slaves? –Rom. 6:15-16

In our natural state we are entirely without any power. –William Law

The friend of God knows that the victory is not his own. It belongs to God. –Hans Denk

With all we've discussed about obedience and producing fruit, a person might think that those who live the Kingdom Life have little appreciation for grace. However, just the opposite is true. Only the Christian who exerts himself in running the race of life, who strives to enter the narrow gate, who disciplines his body so as not to be disapproved, who daily examines himself and confesses his sins—only he can fully appreciate how wonderful and essential God's grace truly is. For he knows only too well that even in our best human efforts, we are never deserving of eternal life.

But those in the Kingdom Life know grace is a costly thing. Dietrich Bonhoeffer explains it this way: "Costly grace is the gospel which must be sought again and again and again, the gift which must be asked for, the door at which a man must knock. Such grace is costly because it calls us to follow, and it is grace because it calls us to follow Jesus Christ. It is costly because it costs a man his life, and it is grace because it gives a man the only true life. It is costly because it condemns sin, and grace because it justifies the sinner. Above all, it is costly because it cost God the life of his Son: 'Ye were bought at a price,' and what has cost God much cannot be cheap for us. Above all, it is grace because God did not reckon his Son too dear a price to pay for our life, but delivered him up for us."[105]

Grace is indeed costly. We insult God when we take His grace for granted and treat it as something automatically owed to us because we once prayed the sinner's prayer. Hebrews tells us, "Anyone who has rejected Moses' law dies without mercy on the testimony of two or three witnesses. Of how much worse punishment, do you suppose, will he be thought worthy who has trampled the Son of God underfoot, counted the blood of the covenant by which he was sanctified a common thing, and insulted the Spirit of grace?" (Heb 10:28-29).

Bonhoeffer writes, "Cheap grace is the deadly enemy of our Church. We are fighting today for costly grace. Cheap grace means grace sold on the market like cheapjacks' wares. The sacraments, the forgiveness of sin, and the consolations of religion are thrown away at cut-rate prices. Grace is represented as the Church's inexhaustible treasury, from which she showers blessings with generous hands, without asking questions or fixing limits. Grace without price; grace without cost! The essence of grace, we suppose, is that the account has been paid in advance. And because it has been paid, everything can be had for nothing."[106]

In the Kingdom Life, we don't imagine that we can earn our salvation or that we are so good we deserve heaven. Rather we discipline ourselves and obey our Lord because we appreciate how much our salvation cost God. We treasure grace as a precious thing, and we reject cheap grace—which is often no more than a license to sin. We refuse to treat the blood of our dear Savior as a common thing.

Bonhoeffer continues, "Cheap grace means the justification of sin without the justification of the sinner. Grace alone does everything, they say, and so everything can remain as it was before. . . . The world goes on in the same old way, and we are still sinners 'even in the best life' as Luther said." Bonhoeffer adds sarcastically, "Well, then let the Christian live like the rest of the world! Let him model himself on the world's standards in every sphere of life! Let him not presumptuously aspire to live a life under grace that differs from his old life under sin! That was the heresy of the enthusiasts, the Anabaptists, and their kind! Let the Christian beware of rebelling against the free and boundless grace of God and desecrating it!"[107]

We demonstrate our appreciation for God's costly grace by not treating Christ's blood as something cheap. "Cheap grace is the preaching of forgiveness without requiring repentance, baptism without church discipline, and communion without confession,"[108] as Bonhoeffer explains. Those in the Kingdom Life want nothing to do with grace without discipleship and without the cross.

Bonhoeffer correctly observes, "Cheap grace therefore amounts to a denial of the living Word of God, in fact, a denial of the Incarnation of the Word of God."[109]

43

Are You Ready for the Kingdom Life?

The hour will come when you shall desire one day—yes, one hour—for the amendment of your life, and I know not whether you will obtain it. –Thomas á Kempis

His children are not his real, true sons and daughters until they think like Him, feel with Him, judge as he judges, are at home with Him, and without fear before Him because He and they mean the same thing, love the same things, seek the same ends. – George MacDonald

In 281 BC, the Greek king Pyrrhus decided to invade Italy, put down the upstart Roman power, and carve out an empire for himself. His chief adviser, a man named Cineas, asked him what he intended to do once all of that was done. "Why, we will then live the rest of our lives in ease," Pyrrhus replied. "We will enjoy ourselves and have good times with our friends."

Cineas then astutely asked, "Why then, your majesty, don't we simply do that now—live in ease and enjoy ourselves?"[110]

We should all ask ourselves a similar question. What do we look forward to doing in eternity? I can't answer for you, but I'm looking forward to being in the presence of God, worshiping Him, praising Him, obeying Him, and doing whatever heavenly work Christ has in mind for me. Perhaps you would answer similarly.

Why then don't we simply do that now?

Ready, Aim, Surrender!

You and I have traveled quite a ways together since the account of the missionary traveling in Tibet. He unwittingly saved his life by putting love above his own interests. As Jesus says, "Whoever desires to save his life will lose it, but whoever loses his life for My sake will find it" (Matt. 16:25). Do we have the faith to completely lose ourselves in Christ Jesus? We're not talking about artificial surrender, but the real thing. We're talking about living the Kingdom Life that thousands of Christian pilgrims have lived before us.

As missionary E. Stanley Jones puts it, "The moment of the great choice has come—a decision that will decide all other decisions down the line—a master decision."[111] Our one solemn commitment to live the Kingdom Life will determine what choices we make for the rest of our lives. A. W. Tozer expressed it this way: "I would emphasize this one committal, this one great volitional act which establishes the heart's intention to gaze forever upon Jesus."[112] John Wesley made such a commitment as a young man. He wrote in his journal, "Instantly I resolved to dedicate all my life to God, all my thoughts, words, and actions—so that every part of my life (not some only) would be a sacrifice to God."[113] The rest is history.

We've discussed the secrets of the Kingdom Life. So what's the next step? If you're willing, the next step is to make a formal commitment to God to live such a life. Obviously, just making a commitment to God isn't in itself going to radically change any of us. But it's important to communicate to God our intentions. Surely none of us will live the Kingdom Life unless we deliberately commit to do so and unless we receive God's blessings and power.

The Joyous Commitment

Exactly what kind of commitment should we make? Various spiritual writers through the centuries have described the needed commitment in different ways. William Law describes it in this manner:

> Let it now be a rule of your life, to look up to God in all your actions, to do everything in His fear, and to abstain from everything that is not according to His will. It must be the settled purpose and intention of your heart, to will nothing, design nothing, do nothing, except so far as you have reason to believe that it is the will of God that you should so desire, design, and do. You are therefore to consider yourself as a person who has no other business in the world but to be that which God requires you to be.[114]

Samuel Logan Brengle describes it as making a commitment to live each day as though you were going to die that evening:

> If you knew you had to die at sunset tonight, what would you do? You would give yourself to God. If you had any grudges against any of your neighbors, you would give them up, and if you had the opportunity you would ask them to forgive you for hating them, even though they had wronged you or some of your friends. You would not stop to think how they would treat you. You would not care. You would feel it your business to get right, and you would leave them with God. If you had robbed any man, you would try to restore to him what was his. If you had any selfish plans, or ambitions, they would sink into mole hills before the mighty mountains of eternity, and you would give them up quickly.[115]

Francis of Sales describes the commitment in these words:

> From here on, God will be the sole object of your thoughts. No more will you give your mind to ideas

> that are displeasing to God. All the days of your life you will dwell upon the greatness of His goodness, so lovingly poured out upon you. You have forsaken, rejected, detested and renounced all willful sin forever. You have dedicated and consecrated your heart, body, and soul—with everything pertaining to them, to the service and love of God. You should often repeat to yourself with heart and voice these words, "I am not my own. Whether I live or whether I die, I am the Lord's. There is no longer any me or mine. Rather, my 'me' is Jesus, my 'mine' is His."[116]

Don't Make the Commitment Lightly

Those are lofty goals indeed! And since this is such a major commitment, it is not something to make rashly. Too many Christians have fallen into the habit of hastily making promises and commitments to God—perhaps while under the conviction of fiery preaching—that they soon forget. No commitment to God should ever be made lightly or in a momentary emotional rush.

However, if God has brought you to the point where you're ready to embrace the Kingdom Life, I encourage you to make the commitment. You might want to use the language of the spiritual writers I quoted above. Or you might want to compose your own. Or you can use the suggested one below:

> Father, from hereafter I want to love you with all of my heart, soul, mind, and strength. I want to love my neighbor as myself. I want my life to be fully hidden in that of your Son's. It is the intention of my heart to will nothing and to do nothing unless it is in accordance with your will. I know that without Christ I can do nothing, but that with Him I can do all things.
>
> Father, I want to live the Kingdom Life, a life where I seek first your kingdom in all I do. I want to love

each and every commandment you've given. Please give me the power to live this life. I commit to you that, with your help, I will deny myself daily and give my life wholly to you. Yet, Father, I know that as a descendant of Adam I will stumble many times in this endeavor. When that happens, with your help I will pick myself up, repent, and continue on living a life surrendered to you. In Jesus' name. Amen.

The Potion in the Bottle

Leonard Scheimer, 1527

The ungodly are saying that we drink something out of a bottle, and the devil himself has no idea what is in that bottle. They say whoever drinks from the bottle isn't happy with ordinary life any more. He acts differently and has no concern for money or life.

Well, you people without God, I want to explain it to you. I will let you call it a "bottle." And it is true; the devil doesn't know what is in that "bottle"! And it is true that whoever drinks from that "bottle" becomes a different person!

The drink in this bottle is simply the smashed, beaten, ground up, and troubled heart, crushed by the mortar called "the cross." Yes, it is such a powerful "bottle" to drink from, that whenever someone drinks of it, he becomes another person, and his neighbors take notice.[117]

Leonard Scheimer was an early Anabaptist leader, who died for his faith a few months after writing the passage above.

Notes

1 http://www.dictionary.com.
2 GAMEO, (*Was geredt sey*, Jones, 23).
3 William Law, *The Spirit of Love*, Kindle edition, 8021.
4 Francis of Sales, *Introduction to the Devout Life*, Kindle edition, 497367.
5 John Wesley, "A Blow at the Root or Christ Stabbed in the House of His Friends," vol. 10, *The Works of John Wesley, Third Ed.* (Peabody, Mass.: Hendrickson Publishers, 1991),367-369, condensed.
6 Anonymous, *The Kneeling Christian*, Kindle edition, 1026.
7 Henry Scougal, *The Life of God in the Soul of Man*, Kindle edi tion, 560.
8 Clement of Alexandria, quoted in *A Dictionary of Early Christian Beliefs* (Peabody, Mass.: Hendrickson Publishers, 1998), 295.
9 J. C. Ryle, *Practical Christianity*, Kindle edition, 1210.
10 Ibid.
11 William Law, *A Serious Call to a Devout and Holy Life*, Kindle edition, 4917.
12 Samuel Logan Brengle, *Heart Talks on Holiness*, Kindle edition, 44.
13 Justin Martyr, quoted in *A Dictionary of Early Christian Beliefs*, 56.
14 http://www.dictionary.com.
15 *The Kneeling Christian*, 1656.
16 Law, *A Serious Call to a Devout and Holy Life*, 1744, 1747.
17 Law, *A Serious Call to a Devout and Holy Life*, 2510.
18 Law, *A Serious Call to a Devout and Holy Life*, 2512.
19 Tertullian, quoted in *A Dictionary of Early Christian Beliefs*, 532.
20 Matthew Henry, *Directions for Daily Communion with God*, Kindle edition, 287.
21 Scougal, *The Life of God in the Soul of Man*, 398.
22 Law, *A Serious Call to a Devout and Holy Life*, 4878.
23 Andrew Murray, *The Deeper Christian Life*, Kindle edition, 8891.
24 Law, *A Serious Call to a Devout and Holy Life*, 2654.
25 Law, *A Serious Call to a Devout and Holy Life*, 4359, 4364.
26 Henry, *Directions for Daily Communion with God*, 224.
27 Law, *A Serious Call to a Devout and Holy Life*, 2639.
28 Anthony Bloom, *God and Man* (New York: St. Vladimir's Seminary Press, 1983), 106.

29 Clement of Alexandria, quoted in *The Pilgrim Road* (Amberson, PA: Scroll Publishing Co., 1991), 343.
30 Dirk Philips, *Early Anabaptist Spirituality* (Mahwah, New Jersey: Pau list Press, 1994), 200.
31 Henry Scougal, *The Life of God in the Soul of Man*, Kindle edition, 40.
32 J. C. Ryle, *Practical Christianity*, Kindle edition, 925.
33 George Otis, Jr., *The God They Never Knew* (Van Nuys: Bible Voice, Inc., 1978), 148.
34 Isaac Watts, *A Burning and a Shining Light* (Grand Rapids: Wm. B. Eerdmans Publishing Co., 1987), 79.
35 Brengle, *Heart Talks on Holiness*, 997.
36 Law, *A Treatise on Christian Perfection*, 16179.
37 Richard of St. Victor, *On the Trinity*, Kindle edition, 14679.
38 George MacDonald, *Unspoken Sermons, Series I, II, and III*, Kindle edition,1360.
39 John Wesley, *Sermon LXXXVIII* (condensed).
40 A. W. Tozer, *Pursuit of God*, Kindle edition, 1051.
41 Wesley, *Sermon LXXXVIII* (condensed).
42 http://www.huffingtonpost.com/2013/09/23/beauty-products_n_3975209.html.
43 Wesley, *Sermon LXXXVIII* (condensed).
44 Ryle, *Practical Christianity*, 1544.
45 Tozer, *Pursuit of God*, 675.
46 Brengle, *Heart Talks on Holiness*, 1327.
47 Law, *A Serious Call to a Devout and Holy Life*, 1336.
48 William Law, *A Treatise on Christian Perfection*, Kindle edition, 15757.
49 Wesley, *The Complete Sermons*, Kindle edition, 11471,11476, condensed.
50 http://www.dictionary.com.
51 Wesley, *The Complete Sermons*, 250.
52 John Wesley, "The Nature, Design, and General Rules of the United Societies," http://archive.org/stream/cihm_38065#page/n5/mode/2up.
53 Brengle, *Heart Talks on Holiness*, 1428.
54 Scougal, *The Life of God in the Soul of Man*, 161.
55 *The Kneeling Christian*, 1707.
56 Andrew Murray, *With Christ in the School of Prayer*, Kindle edition, 13231.
57 Law, *A Serious Call to a Devout and Holy Life*, 3582.
58 Law, *The Spirit of Love*, 8026, 8013, 8009, condensed.
59 Wesley, *The Complete Sermons*, 4935.
60 http://www.gospelway.com/christianlife/meekness.php.
61 Thomas á Kempis, *The Imitation of Christ*, Kindle edition, 1522.
62 Francis of Assisi, *Francis and Clare, The Complete Works* (New York: Paulist Press, 1982), 32.
63 Law, *A Serious Call to a Devout and Holy Life*, 3506-3512.

64 MacDonald, *Unspoken Sermons, Series I, II, and III*, 1701-1702.
65 Alexander Campbell, *Christian Baptist*, February 11, 1826.
66 http://www.dictionary.com.
67 Law, *A Serious Call to a Devout and Holy Life*, 4309.
68 Law, *A Treatise on Christian Perfection*, 15857.
69 Law, *A Serious Call to a Devout and Holy Life*, 4504.
70 Verwer, *No Turning Back*, 29.
71 MacDonald, *Unspoken Sermons, Series I, II, and III*, condensed.
72 Rom. 16:5; 1 Cor. 16:19; Col. 4:15; Philem. 2, 22.
73 http://www.globalrichlist.com.
74 http://www.dictionary.com.
75 Wesley, *The Complete Sermons*, 18509.
76 Matt. 5:35.
77 Ibid.
78 Ibid.
79 Matt. 5:36.
80 Ibid.
81 Ibid.
82 Matt. 28:19.
83 This is described throughout the Book of Acts and many of Paul's epistles.
84 1 Cor. 12:28.
85 Heb. 13:17.
86 Matt. 28:20.
87 Rom. 16:1-6.
88 Jas. 5:16; Col. 4:12; Acts 12:5; Rom. 15:30,31.
89 Matt. 5:9.
90 1 Thess. 5:11.
91 Heb. 13:2.
92 1 Cor. 12:28.
93 Jas. 1:27.
94 1 Thess. 3:1-3; 5:11.
95 1 Cor. 12:4-11.
96 Clement of Alexandria in *A Dictionary of Early Christian Beliefs*, 507.
97 "If God asked you 'Why should I let you into Heaven?', what would you say?," quoted at https://answers.yahoo.com/question/index?qid=20 0.61001132013AAi4uRD.
98 Tertullian in *A Dictionary of Early Christian Beliefs*, 9.
99 Ibid.
100 http://www.alanknox.net/2011/01/the-christians-support-not-only-their-own-poor-but-ours-as-well.
101 Francis of Sales, *Introduction to the Devout Life*, 330576.
102 Austin Warren, in Introduction to *William Law* (New York: Paulist Press, 1978), 14.

103 Wesley, *The Complete Sermons*, 18234.
104 Wesley, *The Complete Sermons*, 18226.
105 Dietrich Bonhoeffer, *The Cost of Discipleship* (New York: Macmillan Publishing Co., 1937), 47, 48.
106 Ibid., 45.
107 Ibid., 46.
108 Ibid.
109 Ibid.
110 Law, quoting Plutarch, in *A Treatise on Christian Perfection*, 16130.
111 E. Stanley Jones, *Abundant Living* (Jove Publications, Inc., 1942), 22.
112 Tozer, *Pursuit of God*, 808.
113 Wesley, *A Treatise on Christian Perfection,* Kindle edition, 48.
114 Law, *A Serious Call to a Devout and Holy Life*, 3601,4611, 4615.
115 Brengle, *Heart Talks on Holiness*, 198.
116 Francis of Sales, *Introduction to the Devout Life*, 66568, 70801, 623828.
117 Leonard Scheimer, adapted from *Spiritual Life in Anabaptism* (Scottsdale, PA:Herald Press, 1995), 217.

THE PILGRIM ROAD

The Pilgrim Road is a unique devotional handbook that collects together the best insights, reflections, and practical counsel of the early Christians. During the 2nd and 3rd centuries A.D., Christianity was an illegal, persecuted religion throughout most of the civilized world. In many ways, this was a blessing. That's because persecution culled out superficial Christians and those who were not willing to make sacrifices for Christ.

The passionate Christianity of those early centuries can bless today's Christians as well. That's because the spiritual pilgrims of those centuries have left us a rich legacy of vibrant writings that provide keen insight on how to walk down the pilgrim road.

It is better for me to die on behalf of Jesus Christ, then to reign over all the ends of the earth. Ignatius

The best riches are poverty of desires. Clement of Alexandria

The business of a Christian is nothing else than to be ever preparing for death. Irenaeus

We are as close to the ears of God as we are to the commandments of God. Tertullian